It's time to fight back! Christia~~n~~
the West, martyred in the Mid~~d~~
East. Global hypertension is out o~~f control while most western~~
Christians passively watch and worry. Is this God's plan for
us? Or do we have a higher calling? In *The Weapon of Prayer*
David Ireland winsomely but urgently calls us from being indifferent spiritual wimps to becoming heroic warriors by using the
weapon God has given us: prayer—*"For the weapons of our warfare are not human weapons, but are made powerful by God for
tearing down strongholds"* (2 Cor. 10:4). I've been stirred to be a
kneeling warrior. You will be too.

—DAVID E. SCHROEDER, EdD
PRESIDENT, PILLAR COLLEGE
TRUTH IN EDUCATION

I've had the privilege of being with Dr. Ireland as he has ministered to members of the New York Giants at their pregame
chapel services. His godly character, knowledge of the scriptures, and skillful presentations of God's Word encouraged and
strengthened the men. "Ask him back" is the request I hear regularly from the athletes after Dr. Ireland's visits.

—GEORGE McGOVERN
NY GIANTS AND NY YANKEES, CHAPEL LEADER

Very seldom will you find an individual with so much knowledge of the Word and an equally tremendous passion for Jesus.

—KURT WARNER
RETIRED NFL QUARTERBACK AND HOST, *THE MOMENT*

There is too much passivity in the church. Christians have
embraced a distortion of God's sovereignty and abandoned the
battle. In *The Weapon of Prayer* Dr. David Ireland confronts
this passivity. As I read this book on Easter Sunday 2015, I was
convicted, inspired, and motivated to enter the battle with a
newfound vigor and courage. The kingdom of God will advance
in and through your life as a result of this book.

—DR. RON WALBORN
DEAN, ALLIANCE THEOLOGICAL SEMINARY, NYACK COLLEGE,
NYACK, NEW YORK

Dr. Ireland knows his way around the courtroom of God. This book will prove it, and your life will show it.

—LEONARD SWEET
AUTHOR, FROM TABLET TO TABLE
PROFESSOR, DREW UNIVERSITY, GEORGE FOX UNIVERSITY,
AND TABOR COLLEGE
CREATOR, PREACHTHESTORY.COM

In *The Weapon of Prayer* David Ireland again reminds the body of Christ of the dynamism that prayer is for the believer. In this day of increased conflict where the sword seems to be the weapon of choice, David renews our call to the only weapon in our arsenal—effective prayer! This book is a call to every disciple to quit standing on the sidelines just observing and hoping you don't get drawn into the fray. When the headlines frustrate and frighten us, there is something we can do. We can draw out our weapon of prayer.

—MIKE SERVELLO
FOUNDER AND CEO, COMPASSION COALITION, UTICA, NEW YORK

As a pastoral leader who operates with a strong prophetic gifting and insightful revelation, Dr. David Ireland is a sought-after voice in the realm of prayer. Well versed in Scripture and in life experience, he unwraps the often bewildering concept of prayer in such a way that anyone can benefit—not only in his speaking, but also in his counsel and writing. With *The Weapon of Prayer* Dr. Ireland does it again. Inciting and illuminating, the often overlooked and misunderstood facet of prayer as a weapon of spiritual warfare comes alive.

—PIERRE DU PLESSIS
LEAD PASTOR, THE FATHER'S HOUSE, ROCHESTER, NEW YORK

When I began to read *The Weapon of Prayer*, I was sitting on a ferry on a beautiful morning on my way to work. When the ferry docked, I disembarked and hurried to my office where I sat enthralled, unable to put it down until I had finished it. This work is full of inspirational stories built on the bedrock of excellent theology and insightful exegesis. Dr. David Ireland has challenged my understanding and confronted my practice.

He has pulled together for me the threads of nearly thirty years of my personal and ministry prayer experiences, to present to me a fresh revelation of what this core practice is all about. My relationship to God in prayer has been changed today, in substance, focus, no doubt results, and almost certainly duration. Dr. David is a man of passionate integrity and fierce intelligence, who loves the Word, walks in step with the Spirit, treasures his family, and loves his church. He is a leader this generation needs to listen to.

—MIKE GRIFFITHS
NATIONAL LEADER, ELIM CHURCH OF NEW ZEALAND

When Concerts of Prayer Greater New York desires to display an awesome praying pastor, we often point to pastor David Ireland of Christ Church. He models prayer and boldly leads his congregation through main prayer disciplines that are often neglected. Dr. David Ireland is a significant leader in the body of Christ.

—DIMAS SALABERRIOS
PRESIDENT, CONCERTS OF PRAYER GREATER NEW YORK

When I started to read *The Weapon of Prayer*, I was immediately captured by the introduction. Dr. Ireland is a master at drawing people into a conversation and opportunity for deeper reflection. Prayer is one of those topics that needs a fresh enticement to overcome the unfortunate inertia around the subject. Nothing we can do is more important than prayer; therefore, nothing is more important for us to study to enhance its practice. Dr. Ireland attempts the near impossible—to inform and challenge us toward a prayer-focused life. Thankfully *The Weapon of Prayer* succeeds in motivating its readers to pray, which strategically results in advancing the precious gospel of our Lord Jesus Christ.

—TOM HORN, PhD
DIRECTOR OF LEADER DEVELOPMENT, THE NAVIGATORS

Dr. David Ireland is an amazing apostolic gift with such a prolific mind. His gift is displayed in what he has built and established and maintained. There are those who haven't built anything and cannot teach "it." There are those who teach "it" but haven't built anything. There are those who have built "it" and can't teach "it"; but there are those who have built "it" and teach "it." David Ireland has built "it" and is teaching "it." God has raised him to teach this generation how to war through prayer. *The Weapon of Prayer* is a tool in the hands of the believer that, when used, will project incredible visible results against the world of the devil. We know that testimonies of notable victories will emerge from this tool.

—BISHOP TUDOR BISMARK
JABULA NEW LIFE MINISTRIES, HARARE, ZIMBABWE

You can't read this book without becoming better trained and better motivated in strategic prayer. I have known Dr. Ireland for over ten years and each time I'm around him, something good is stirred inside of me. I pray that the same thing happens to you as you read *The Weapon of Prayer*.

—WARREN BIRD, PHD
COAUTHOR, *UNLEASHING THE WORD: REDISCOVERING THE PUBLIC READING OF SCRIPTURE*

*the*

# WEAPON OF
# PRAYER

### DAVID D. IRELAND, PhD

CHARISMA
HOUSE

Most CHARISMA HOUSE BOOK GROUP products are available at special quantity discounts for bulk purchase for sales promotions, premiums, fund-raising, and educational needs. For details, write Charisma House Book Group, 600 Rinehart Road, Lake Mary, Florida 32746, or telephone (407) 333-0600.

THE WEAPON OF PRAYER by David D. Ireland
Published by Charisma House
Charisma Media/Charisma House Book Group
600 Rinehart Road
Lake Mary, Florida 32746
www.charismahouse.com

Cover design by Justin Evans

Visit the author's website at www.davidireland.org.

Library of Congress Cataloging-in-Publication Data:
Ireland, David, 1961-
  The weapon of prayer / by David D. Ireland. -- First edition.
    pages cm
  Includes bibliographical references and index.
  ISBN 978-1-62998-676-0 (trade paper : alk. paper) -- ISBN 978-1-62998-677-7 (e-book : alk. paper)
 1.  Prayer--Christianity. 2.  Spiritual warfare.  I. Title.

  BV210.3.I745 2015
  248.3'2--dc23

                                 2015016629

First edition

15 16 17 18 19 — 9 8 7 6 5 4 3 2 1
Printed in the United States of America

*This book is lovingly dedicated to every person who desires to teach others the art of prayer.*

# CONTENTS

# FOREWORD

I WAS NOT PREPARED for how good this book would be. Knowing that the author, Dr. David Ireland, had written a brilliant book on prayer—*The Kneeling Warrior*—I wondered if he could match the previous one.

He did, only more so. This book is a sequel, a beautiful continuation of what we read previously. It is completely fresh and filled with some of the most inspiring stories I have ever come across.

You won't be able to put this book down.

If *The Kneeling Warrior* inspired you to pray, *The Weapon of Prayer* will do this even more so. In my foreword to *The Kneeling Warrior* I predicted that it would become a classic, ranking alongside the greatest books on prayer. And yet David has done it again, writing another amazing treatise on prayer. Dr. Ireland has an original mind. Demonstrating on every page that prayer is a *weapon* against the world, the flesh, and

the devil, he has shown that the youngest Christian can succeed in this war. That said, the most mature Christian will be
inspired all over again to never, never, never give up praying.

Prayer as our secret weapon is both offensive—invading
Satan's territory, and defensive—how to respond when under
attack. You will be following in the steps of Jesus, the greatest
Man of prayer that ever was, whose secret prayer life you
will want to emulate when you read this book. If Jesus, the
God-Man, needed to pray, how much more you and I?

Get ready to be encouraged, thrilled, and humbled. Read
and listen to the voice of the Holy Spirit. Hear a pastor's
heartbeat. What the people of Christ Church in Montclair
and Rockaway, New Jersey, get to receive all the time, can be
your feast as you read this wonderful book.

> Come, my soul, thy suit prepare.
> Jesus loves to answer prayer;
> He Himself has bid thee pray,
> Therefore will not say thee nay.
>
> Thou art coming to a King,
> Large petitions with thee bring;
> For His grace and power are such
> None can ever ask too much.[1]
>
> —John Newton (1725–1807)

—Dr. R. T. Kendall
Minister, Author, *It Ain't Over Till It's Over* and *Holy Fire*
Westminster Chapel (1977–2002)

# INTRODUCTION

I COULDN'T BELIEVE IT. I'd just been rear-ended by a long, black, shiny hearse.

Fortunately no one was hurt. The undertaker was gracious and apologetic as he braced himself for an expletive-filled blast from me. That's typically what New York drivers do in situations like this.

Instead I calmed him down. "Is this how you get new customers?" I joked while staring at his black-on-black outfit.

He chuckled. "I was just running a few errands."

As we exchanged insurance information and the other particulars, I thought, "A hearse can be used to run errands?" Although normal to him, it was strange to me.

Then it dawned on me: the company car of funeral homes *is* a hearse. So I guess it makes sense.

That kind of disconnect is what happens when most Christians think about prayer being used as a weapon. It almost seems sacrilegious to mention the words *prayer* and *weapon* in the same sentence. Yet when you probe deeper, you will see that prayer was Jesus's weapon of choice whenever He had to go toe to toe with Satan. It was normal to Him. Prayer was His company vehicle—a weapon wielded to navigate and defeat the enemy.

Consider what Jesus said to one of His strongest disciples, Simon Peter: "Simon, Simon, Satan has asked to sift all of you like wheat. But I have prayed for you, Simon, that your faith may not fail" (Luke 22:31–32). Satan was granted his wish to launch an all-out attack against Peter, yet Jesus did not quiver or speak to Peter in some kind of frightened tone. I can envision our Lord standing flatfooted as He asserted, "I have prayed for you." It's like He was saying, "I have used the weapon of prayer, Peter. Relax. All will be well."

Prayer was the backbone and foundation of the ministry and life of Jesus. Before every major decision, such as choosing the twelve apostles, He prayed (Luke 6:12). Surrounding every significant experience, such as water baptism, Jesus prayed (Luke 3:21). When He needed to recharge, He prayed (Luke 5:16). When He needed to simply relax and commune with God, He prayed (Mark 1:35). Prayer was the mainstay of Jesus's diet. He believed in prayer. He depended on prayer. He practiced prayer. He taught on prayer.

Since Jesus used prayer as a weapon, a number of inescapable conclusions must be drawn. The first is that the Christian walk is a warfare walk. We cannot sit idly by and expect to saunter into heaven loaded down with God's promises. We must fight our dreaded adversaries in a most skillful way. This is how we are going to fulfill the Great Commission, bring deliverance to the captives, build a hedge of protection around our families, and put Satan on the defense by taking an offensive posture as it relates to spiritual warfare. None of this will be accomplished unless we become skillful with the weapon of prayer. This brings us to a second inescapable conclusion: we need to become skillful using prayer as a weapon.

This book will teach you how.

## THIS BOOK'S PROMISE

There are a number of books on the market today about prayer. A few even talk about spiritual warfare. An even smaller number touch on the need to use prayer as a weapon. In this book I provide in-depth training and a solid biblical game plan for how to use prayer as Jesus often used it: as a weapon. I spell out the *how* of it with solid evangelical theology and lots of practical stories designed to make you a skilled soldier in the army of the Lord.

If you desire to learn how to defend yourself and your family and how to take hold of your inheritance through prayer, this book is for you. It will help you answer the following questions:

- How is prayer a weapon?
- How can I use the weapon of prayer to protect and shield my family?
- How can I use the weapon of prayer to take new territory for the glory of God?
- What are the practical sides of spiritual warfare?
- How can I maintain a healthy balance between faith and action?

- How can I fulfill my potential as a soldier in the army of the Lord?

There was no doubt in the mind of Jesus as to the sufficiency of prayer when it came to safeguarding Peter's life and legacy. And if prayer was all Jesus needed to bring Satan's attack to a screeching halt, then we need to believe that too—and understand the intricacies surrounding the use of prayer as a weapon.

Jesus's prayer dismantled Satan's intent. It disabled his power. It destroyed the hope of Satan's plans against Peter. Prayer was Jesus's chosen weapon, and it must be yours too. Just as a soldier goes through boot camp to learn how to skillfully use his weapons, this book will be your spiritual boot camp for mastering your greatest weapon—prayer.

*Chapter 1*

# YOU MUST FIGHT!

On Tuesday, June 24, 2014, a young mother was attacked and viciously beaten in front of her two-year-old son and a dozen adults. The attacker—a coworker at the neighborhood McDonald's—broke Catherine Ferreira's nose and repeatedly punched and kicked her due to alleged rumors and workplace gossip.

The more shocking crime, in my estimation, was a moral one. Not one of the onlookers lifted a finger to help. Instead they whipped out their cell phones to videotape the beating that resulted in a concussion, two black eyes, and numerous cuts and bruises. The fifty-four-second video of the beating recorded one person who left the sidelines to help the victim—Catherine's two-year-old son, Xzavion Ortiz.[1]

Everything within this two-year-old drove him to leave the sidelines and jump into the fray. Xzavion's brave heart compelled him to lay blows on the larger woman assaulting his mother. His tiny feet could do no damage to the assailant, but he kicked her anyway. He knew it was wrong to sit on the sidelines. The pocket-size warrior concluded that he must fight. It was *right* to fight! It would be wrong *not* to fight. And it would be a moral crime to watch the attack from the sidelines.

Had I been one of the "innocent bystanders" watching this poor woman get pummeled, I would be embarrassed to show my face in public. I would be even more embarrassed to tell anyone I had watched the beating from the safety of the sidelines.

Yet these bystanders showed no embarrassment or remorse. Before Catherine reached the hospital, the cowardly spectators had brazenly uploaded the video footage to their

Facebook pages and other social media outlets. Their outrageous behavior—doing nothing to help a woman in danger and instead videotaping the event as it happened—reflects the ethical blindness of their souls.

A lot of people share my moral outrage and righteous anger toward these sideliners. Yet when it comes to spiritual warfare, many of us are guilty of the same crime of indifference. This unresponsiveness to the need for prayer creates lukewarm Christ-followers, weak churches, and an unattractive Christian faith. Since prayer is the wellspring of excitement and spiritual passion for the Lord, prayerlessness does the opposite. Sitting on the sideline is not just a moral crime; it is also a spiritual crime. A spiritually indifferent person distracts fighters embroiled in the battle because their lack of concern is felt each time the fighter looks to the sideliners for help. Help never comes. If sideliners just inched closer to the fray, hope would be kindled in the heart of the battle-worn saint. Just knowing that others are praying for me buoys my faith.

Prayer is one of the most powerful weapons we've been given. Through it we can thwart Satan's purposes, break through hellish hordes bent on hindering the will of God, and drive our flag—the flag of the conquering Savior—into the ground, declaring, "The Lord God reigns over this generation!" But becoming a kneeling warrior cannot happen by sitting on the sidelines. It demands the same kind of militancy little Xzavion demonstrated. Paul was inspired by the Holy Spirit to command every Christ-follower to put on the full armor of God and engage in the spiritual war. (See Ephesians 6:10–18.) You must fight!

# NEUTRALITY IS A SPIRITUAL CRIME

Satan is attacking people and purpose, but many believers have chosen to remain as "innocent bystanders" on the scene, detached and disengaged from his savage assault. However, there's nothing innocent about spiritual neutrality. In the case of Catherine Ferreira the so-called innocent bystanders could not be charged with a civil crime, but in my opinion they are guilty of committing a spiritual crime.

It's this kind of silent indifference that forced Dr. Martin Luther King Jr. to say, "In the end, we will remember not the words of our enemies but the silence of our friends."[2] King wasn't alone in this sentiment. Elie Wiesel, the 1986 Nobel Peace Prize winner, wrote, "I swore never to be silent whenever and wherever human beings endure suffering and humiliation. We must always take sides. Neutrality helps the oppressor, never the victim. Silence encourages the tormentor, never the tormented."[3] Although these two men were speaking specifically to social injustice, the principle still holds true when it comes to spiritual injustice. We must lift up our prayers to the eternal King on behalf of the hurting and the spiritually blind. In this instance silence is not sacred—it's unholy!

Known for his many books on prayer, E. M. Bounds sheds additional light on the impact of prayerlessness. He writes:

> But when it comes to the affairs of the Kingdom, let it be said, at once, that a prayerless man in the Church of God is like a paralyzed organ of the physical body. He is out of place in the communion of saints, out of harmony with God, and out of accord with His purposes for mankind. A prayerless man handicaps the vigor and life of the whole system like a demoralized soldier is a

menace to the force of which he forms part, in the day of battle.[4]

Samuel took this detachment from prayer to another level by labeling prayerlessness as sin. He told the Israelites, "As for me, far be it from me that I should sin against the LORD by failing to pray for you" (1 Sam. 12:23). From this Old Testament prophet we learn that it is sinful at times not to pray for others. It's sinful not to use the weapon of prayer to ward off the enemy's attacks against humanity. It is sin for us to live on the sidelines, detached from the battle. Samuel was teaching the people of his day the same important lesson we must learn today: prayerlessness is sin.

It's hard to admit that prayerlessness is sin if you limit the scope of sin to actions. Sin goes beyond completed actions and includes attitudes and dispositions of the heart. When we shirk our responsibility to pray, whatever the reason, we are guilty of committing a sin—a sin of omission.

Samuel lived by this principle because he said, "Far be it from me." This personal standard helps preserve a healthy perspective and practice toward intercessory prayer. He did not want to be guilty of allowing an attitude of indifference or neglect to breed in his heart. Such an attitude would infect his prayer life. Samuel's vigilance in prayer prevented the erosion of his prayer life and protected him from living on the sidelines.

Similarly Paul ended his second letter to Timothy by stating, "I have fought the good fight, I have finished the race, I have kept the faith" (2 Tim. 4:7). He was referring to the spiritual fight between good versus evil and the part he was to play as a soldier in the army of the Lord. The apostle was proud of the fact that he did not live his life on the sidelines, disconnected from the fight.

No one is exempt from this fight, not even great leaders such as Paul. Everyone must fight! You're either a willful fighter or a witnessing spectator. The choice is yours. You are either on one side or the other. Even if you don't remember making a choice, you're still involved.

Paul chose. He was very much engaged in the battle—so much so that he intimated the baton was now being passed to Timothy. The obligation to fight for God's purposes for the next generation—Timothy's generation—was now left up to Timothy and his contemporaries.

In the same way, the baton is passed to us. We must fight for the purpose of God for our generation. Sideline living is not for us, no matter how comfortable it may appear. Peter's strong words on this point are: "Keep a cool head. Stay alert. The Devil is poised to pounce, and would like nothing better than to catch you napping. Keep your guard up" (1 Pet. 5:8, THE MESSAGE). Our charge is one of vigilance—to keep a posture of alertness and watchfulness.

## WHAT IT MEANS TO BE VIGILANT

Think of America before and after 9/11 and you'll understand vigilance. Nowadays everyone is on high alert, especially where large crowds gather. The smallest thing, such as a package left unmanned, triggers the evacuation of malls or airports. Threats of violence now fall under the criminal act of terror threats. That's a new crime. A life of vigilance requires new laws, new behaviors, and even new slogans—"If you see something, say something" comes to mind—to reinforce an attitude of watchfulness.

Think too of the impact of the Boston Marathon bombing. Not only did a new slogan come to life in its aftermath too—within one year of the event, about seventy thousand T-shirts were sold with the words "Boston Strong" on them.[5] Its simple message rallied Bostonians and other Americans to be courageous in the face of our new world. That tragedy challenged us to become even more vigilant, especially at major sporting events. As a runner, for example, my attitude toward prerace screenings of my personal belongings is that of welcome. Years ago I would have considered it a nuisance. Today I applaud it. I see it as one aspect of living with a heightened sense of alertness.

Consider what it's like to be in a place where vigilance isn't in place. On a recent trip to Rome to see the Vatican, my wife and I, along with other tourists, walked through the customs checkpoint in Rome's airport undeterred. It was strange. No one stopped us to see our passports, search our bags, or inspect other important documents. In fact, out of my peripheral vision I saw one American question the relaxed customs officer with his rich New England accent.

"Don't you need to check my papers?" he asked. The American's attitude toward vigilance was so ingrained that he was extremely reluctant to pass through the checkpoint without some type of clearance.

The Italian officer smiled and slowly spoke in English for the American to understand his accent: "Get out of here!"

The shocked American struggled to appreciate the lack of vigilance applied in this situation. Yet he listened and walked on briskly to get away from the uncomfortable feeling of life on the sidelines.

# DO YOU HAVE SPIRITUAL HIV?

People who live on the sidelines are complacent. Replacing their spiritual armor with a sporty-looking civilian outfit relaxes them. But the trendy look of these sideliners is the primary symptom of what I call "spiritual HIV," or *high indifference virus*. Just as medical HIV weakens a victim's immune system for warding off infections, the spiritual kind of HIV decreases a warrior's instinct and ability to engage in spiritual battles. His soldier instincts have been compromised. Unbeknownst to himself, he's gone AWOL—absent without official leave.

This infected warrior sits listlessly while his virus-stricken soul weakens from the disease. It breeds further in his soul as the unsuspecting victim adds layers of theological opinion and an assortment of Bible verses to the mix to support his faulty indifference toward spiritual warfare. The more he uses his Bible to shield himself from the war that's raging in the heavenlies, the more the virus takes over his immune system.

The high indifference virus reflects one or more of these four symptoms in its victim: 1) disinterest in the fight, 2) disbelief in the fight, 3) discouraged by the fight, and 4) disdain for the fight.

**Symptom #1: Disinterest in the fight**

The soldier afflicted with spiritual HIV becomes disinterested in and bored with the spiritual fight. He doesn't know he's sick. This virus creates for him a lifestyle of dispassion and disregard not just for the fight but also for the outcome of the fight. He feels there's nothing at stake for him in this fight or believes the stakes are too small to pique his interest.

Nothing could be further from the truth. One of the main aspects of the mission of Jesus was to destroy the works of the devil (1 John 3:8). This includes removing blinders from the minds of people so they can positively respond to God's call to love and serve Him. Jesus was always engaged in the spiritual war. The stakes have not changed!

Admittedly war is never pretty. Fighting is not nice. Yet Scripture declares we are to fight the good fight of faith (1 Tim. 6:12). The Bible positions spiritual warfare as a necessary reality Christians must embrace in order to push back the powers of darkness.

But fighting is not just a necessary action. It is a *loving* action. To the natural mind it seems plausible that natural wars are unavoidable facts of life. Living in the wake of 9/11 and the ongoing existence of Homeland Security, jihadists, cybercrimes, and other contemporary forms of war, there is no question that natural fighting is necessary. Isn't the flip side equally true? Spiritual fighting is also necessary! The stakes are too high to become disinterested. When you participate in the spiritual fight, you join God in loving people into His kingdom. You fight because you love!

### Symptom #2: Disbelief in the fight

A devout Quaker (a denomination known for its peace-loving pacifism and commitment to nonviolence) living in the country with her husband woke up to the sound of something breaking downstairs. She frantically woke her sleeping husband, whispering loudly, "Thomas, I think there's a prowler downstairs. Thee needs to go see."

Thomas got up and grabbed his hunting rifle. As he got to the top of the staircase, sure enough, there was the prowler opposite him below, frozen at the sight of the gun-toting Quaker. Thomas, aiming the gun right at the man, said, "Friend, I mean thee no harm, but thou art standing where I am about to shoot."

Even the peaceful Quaker found a way to fight when confronted with a prowler. He saw peace as an outcome of war. He believed in the fight. A disbelief in the fight would have resulted in loss of property and perhaps even the loss of his life.

While some ailing believers are disinterested in the fight, others living with spiritual HIV disbelieve in the fight altogether. The high indifference virus causes their compromised souls to not see or believe there is a spiritual war happening around them. The irony of this view is that many of these spiritual HIV victims hold to the inerrancy of the Bible, which includes teachings such as, "Therefore put on the full armor of God, so that when the day of evil comes, you may be able to stand your ground" (Eph. 6:13). To one who has never fought spiritually, this verse seems like religious chatter. It has little or no meaning to civilians. Only warriors understand warrior language. But since no warrior's uniform is donned on this person, we must conclude they don't truly believe in the existence of a spiritual war.

Paul's words in this passage to "stand your ground" are taken directly from the military playbook of the Roman army. A Roman centurion had to be the kind of soldier who could be relied upon when the battle was at its darkest point. Then he had to really hold his ground. Paul used *ground* as a metaphor for anything you own and have legal rights to, including ideas, family life, or even God's promises. To *stand your ground* means, then, that you are to be relied upon to maintain your position even when evil is at its darkest point. We are not to allow wickedness to drive us away from the will of God.

When spiritual HIV attacks a soul, the diseased warrior—especially those with little or no experience in spiritual warfare—often concludes, "I'm just having a season of bad luck." He doesn't put two and two together by looking at how the spirit world impacts circumstances in the natural world. Such a partial view of life keeps the diseased soldier functioning as a nonspiritual being—a civilian oblivious to the struggles of war. This flawed perspective cannot be confused with the Judeo-Christian worldview because it's contrary to the Scriptures. If disbelief in the fight causes you to forfeit your ground, such a position cannot be held in good conscience.

Jesus clearly taught that Satan and evil spirits are not metaphorical terms representing evil. They are real beings who have the capability and power to get directly involved in the affairs of human beings. If you hold to a disbelief in the fight, you are also saying, then, that Jesus had a mental breakdown in the desert during His forty days of fasting. To continue this line of reasoning, we must ask: If Satan was a mythical figure or a metaphorical one, who was Jesus confronting in the desert? We see that the Lord's response to the first of Satan's three temptations was, "Man shall not live on bread alone" (Luke 4:4). Afterward Satan led Jesus to a high place, showing Him all the kingdoms of the world in an instant. If Satan was only a symbol of evil, who actually led Jesus to that high place? Was it His imagination? Was He behaving as a schizophrenic?

Quite the contrary. Jesus was not having an emotional breakdown. He was dealing with the dreaded foe—Satan. A disbelief in the fight is a disbelief in Jesus's wilderness experience. You can't have it both ways!

**Symptom #3: Discouraged by the fight**

Three years ago I visited the island of Patmos—the place off the Aegean Sea where the apostle John was imprisoned. (See Revelation 1:9.) In John's day this was a penal island. The Romans exiled prisoners there much like the Island of Alcatraz served as an American federal penitentiary in the mid-1900s. From a grotto located halfway up the side of a hill on Patmos, John received the vision of the apocalypse. To preserve this historic site, the Coptic Orthodox Church built the Monastery of Saint John around the grotto about AD 1088. From the cave, you are able to walk a few steps to the monastery.

While visiting, I encountered a memorable sight when walking into the grotto. A stern-looking Coptic priest stood guard. It was his turn to protect the sanctity of that holy place. Tourists were to be turned away or silenced if they could not honor this sacred space that held an iconic place in history. Photographing the interior of the cave was not allowed.

Although the Coptic priest's duty to preserve that sacred space for coming generations is an extremely important one, he still has to take breaks because fighting is hard work. It demands soldiers function at a constant state of alertness, but if he had to be in high-alert mode constantly, he would feel like a prisoner to the very thing he was guarding. Scheduled breaks refresh him so he can maintain an attitude of alertness over time.

Imagine what would happen if that same priest had to daily guard the grotto without any kind of break or scheduled rotation. Over a period of time such a routine would produce discouragement. So it is with us. If we had to live in a heightened state of alertness every waking moment, we would easily become discouraged in the fight. Some have. Unlike the Coptic priest, those afflicted with spiritual HIV of this sort did not build seasons of respite into their military routine. This cannot help but lead to discouragement over time.

Discouragement bleeds away hope. It reduces one's emotional confidence toward the future. Discouragement stems from many sources. Whether it's the loss of a marriage, the death of a child, the rejection of an application, or our dismissal from a long-standing job, discouragement is like a punch in the breadbasket. It hurts! It's not a nice place to settle emotionally. In fact, it is a very dangerous place to visit, much less settle. It cripples your faith. It wrecks your willingness to fight, even for things that are noble and right.

Some believers are sidelined because they've become discouraged by the fight. They have not learned how to pace themselves when it comes to spiritual warfare. This battle lasts a lifetime. It starts when we're born, and it should take on a new clarity when we're born again. But it ends when we die. The battle ends when heaven's gates open to us.

Until then we must find ways to keep ourselves vigilant and engaged without becoming overwhelmed or decommissioned by discouragement at the length of the war. Just as soldiers need furloughs and the Coptic priests need shifts to guard the grotto, you must pace yourself to be a career soldier. Leading a balanced spiritual life is a surefire way to create respite for yourself. A balanced life must allow for adequate time and attention to be given to relationships, careers, and the mental and physical care of our bodies, in addition to our spiritual development. Admittedly there is tension that exists if we are to build emotionally healthy lives. Yet balance can only be achieved when appropriate care and attention are given to each of these important areas.

A balanced spiritual life must include giving attention to Scripture, prayer, communing with God, and fellowship with other believers. Spending time both privately and publicly in the Word enables you to better know your faith, know God, and know the hope we have in Christ. When you spend time in prayer, your passion for Christ deepens while you gain answers for the challenges of life. Communing with God happens when you practice the disciplines of meditation, solitude, and other biblical habits aimed at keeping your heart pure before God. A healthy spiritual life cannot happen in isolation. We need to fellowship and hang out with other believers. These social interactions create a keen sense of community—a place where encouragement, comfort, and a healthy provocation occurs as a means to grow in our relationship with Christ. These four practices are what caused the early church to be so successful evangelistically and in their personal development (Acts 2:42). Committing to this practice will protect you from contracting spiritual HIV.

Many years ago I tried to teach this principle to a woman in my congregation but was unsuccessful. The woman, whom I'll call Betty, died prematurely because of her imbalanced perspective toward spiritual warfare. She had contracted cancer, but the doctors were optimistic about her chances for recovery. She, on the other hand, wanted instant healing and a clean bill of health. She believed prayer would help her achieve this goal immediately. Despite the fact that her husband was an unbeliever and they were the parents of two young boys, Betty kept up an intense schedule of fasting and prayer.

One Sunday she approached me with the recurring question: "When am I going to get healed?"

This time I pulled away from Bible passages aimed at keeping her perspective balanced. I blurted out, "You have a husband who loves you. Enjoy him! You have two little boys. Enjoy them! Go home and live your life. Bake them some chocolate chip cookies. Have fun! Lead a balanced spiritual life. You can't force God to do anything!"

Betty didn't like my answer. It wasn't spiritual enough for her. So she kept up her impractical fasting regimen. Within a few months I officiated at her funeral service.

Not everything is a fight. Satan is not lurking around every corner waiting to grab you. A warrior's constant alertness does not require a sustained adrenaline rush. The Christian life is not a sixty-yard dash; it's a marathon. Our pace determines how we finish. Strive to finish strong!

## Symptom #4: Disdain for the fight

You may recall the movie *A Few Good Men*. In the film two US Marines are accused of killing Private Santiago, a weaker member of their unit. Lieutenant Daniel Kaffee, played by Tom Cruise, is an attorney in the Navy who was assigned to defend them. He's a cowardly guy whose demeanor expressed a disdain for fighting and the military. Their commanding officer was the hardnose career soldier Colonel Nathan Jessup, played by Jack Nicholson.

A most memorable scene in the movie comes when these two characters clash in the courtroom. Picture the scene with the highly decorated Colonel Jessup sitting in the witness box while the smart-mouthed lawyer Kaffee interrogates him. Jessup's warrior bite snaps out these words:

> Son, we live in a world that has walls, and those walls have to be guarded by men with guns. Who's gonna do it? You? You, Lt. Weinberg [Kaffee's cocounsel]? I have a greater responsibility than you can possibly fathom. You weep for Santiago, and you curse the Marines. You have that luxury. You have the luxury of not knowing what I know: that Santiago's death, while tragic, probably saved lives.
>
> And my existence, while grotesque and incomprehensible to you, saves lives. You don't want the truth because deep down in places you don't talk about at parties, you want me on that wall, you need me on that wall....I have neither the time nor the inclination to explain myself to a man who rises and sleeps under the blanket of the very freedom that I provide and then questions the manner in which I provide it. I would rather you just said thank you and went on your way. Otherwise, I suggest you pick up a weapon and stand a post.[6]

You know a fighter as soon as you see one, and Jessup is a textbook picture of a fighter. He was quick to defend his actions. Overlooking his misguided behavior in the movie, let's just focus on the fact that he was proud of his role. His role on the wall brought security to the people he guarded.

That's what you're called to do in the spiritual realm. Doing this requires that you see fighting as a necessary stepping stone to achieving God's promises.

If you meet someone who has disdain for the fight, rest assured he's suffering from spiritual high indifference virus. Having a disdain for the fight means looking upon spiritual warfare with contempt and scorn. No one starts off with that kind of attitude. When you ask the question, "Why fight?" in a rhetorical manner, you're creating a perspective of hopelessness. This is a surefire way to contract spiritual HIV. Through a series of painful battles, the soldier's question morphs into the declarative statement, *"Don't fight!"* The virus takes hold of his soul, and disdain for the fight spreads.

A flawed theological reasoning often brews to support a disdain for the fight. The thinking goes something such as this: *If God wants it to happen, it will happen. If it's meant to be, it will be.* This faulty view of God, the Scriptures, and spiritual warfare is not new. In fact, it falls under the historic term *antinomianism*. This is the doctrinal notion that because of our salvation relationship in Christ, we are free from the responsibility of obeying God's laws. But you cannot be a victorious warrior if you believe something along these lines: "If God wants me delivered, He will deliver me right here and now. And if He doesn't want me delivered, I won't be."

Antinomianism strips you from bearing any responsibility to work God's Word. The infected fighter no longer believes fighting makes a difference. His disdain makes him a weaponless warrior, like a dog without teeth. His prayers never lead him into the war room. If blessings are not automatically given to this person, he will not search them out through the weapon of prayer.

Just as some people enroll in the US Army because of the fringe benefits—a striking uniform, tuition assistance, and future veteran's benefits—God's army attracts similar inductees. Some people come to Christ only because of the promised salvation and ticket to heaven (which I admit should not be passed over). Yet they have a disdain for fighting.

The calling to be a Christ-follower does not stop with being born again. It progresses to discipleship, which is synonymous with representing Christ on your knees in battle for the souls of men. Paul's words to Timothy hold true for us today: "Join with me in suffering, like a good soldier of Christ Jesus" (2 Tim. 2:3).

Disdain paints a one-sided picture. We welcome God's help, yet we are unwilling to reciprocate. Allegiance should not be one-sided. We must join God on our knees in His battle against evil and wickedness. Disdain for the fight is the same as declaring to God, "Fight Your own battles!" Johann Albrecht Bengel, the Lutheran theologian in the 1700s who greatly influenced John Wesley, suggested, "We do not have God's permission to quit praying until He gives us some answer."[7] It's wrong not to wield the weapon of prayer!

But while spiritual soldiers are not exempt from suffering, as a good General, the Lord accompanies His troops into every battle. He does not leave us alone. That is why David, the warrior king, confidently sang, "Even though I walk through the darkest valley, I will fear no evil, for you are with me; your rod and your staff, they comfort me" (Ps. 23:4). We cannot allow David to sing solo. This verse must be a chorus, your voice harmonizing with his to affirm God's allegiance to His troops.

# ENLIST IN THE FIGHT

As of this writing there is no known cure for HIV. We are grateful, however, for the few pharmaceutical products on the market that extend the lives of those afflicted by this dreaded disease. There is a well-known remedy, however, for spiritual HIV. Repentance treats all four symptoms of the virus that sidelines kneeling warriors. The early church father John Chrysostom said, "Repentance is a medicine which destroys sin, a gift bestowed from heaven, an admirable virtue, a grace exceeding the power of laws."[8]

Whether your warning signs have been disinterest in the fight, disbelief in the fight, discouragement about the fight, or disdain for the fight, repentance is the only antidote you need. Charles G. Finney, an instrumental player in the Second Great Awakening in the United States, guides us in reconnecting with God in prayer. He points out the often overlooked starting point by saying:

> If you have neglected any known duty, and thus lost the spirit of prayer, you must yield first. God has a controversy with you; you have refused obedience to God, and you must retract. You may have forgotten it, but God has not. You must set yourself to recall it to mind and repent. God never will yield or grant you his Spirit, till you repent.[9]

Repentance is unavoidable if you want to move away from the sidelines and reenlist in the fight.

Within the next few minutes, I want you to find a quiet place where you can spend some time in God's throne room. Don't make any request. This is a time for repentance. If you're not quite sure how to get started, use my prayer as a primer to your own plea:

> *Heavenly Father, please forgive me for becoming sidelined in the battle. I know that I've been called to fight the good fight of faith. Forgive me for allowing selfishness and disobedience to run my life.*
>
> *Break me in the right places so I will no longer go astray.*
>
> *Wash me so my attitude is pure and holy.*
>
> *Mold me into a powerful kneeling warrior who continuously prays that Your will be done on earth as it is in heaven.*
>
> *I ask You this in Jesus's name. Amen.*

*Chapter 2*

# ONE POWERFUL WEAPON

Y OU AND I look forward to Thursdays. For most of us, Thursdays—especially Thursday nights—mark the near-start of the weekend. Fun, relaxation, and downtime are about to begin.

But Jesus faced a Thursday that was unusually dark and somber, and not because of a moonless sky. It was the Thursday before Good Friday—the night before the Lamb of God was to be sacrificed on Golgotha's hill. Jesus conceded His soul was "overwhelmed with sorrow to the point of death" (Matt. 26:38).

And yet despite His distress, Jesus was very much preoccupied with the welfare of His disciples. We know that He hosted a Last Supper for them, teaching them about the significance of the bread and wine that symbolized His body and blood that would soon be given for them. (See Matthew 26:26–29.) We know He washed their feet, telling them His example of service was one for them to follow. (See John 13:1–17.) We know that after dinner, He voiced a full-length prayer that marked His concern for the disciples after His departure. (See John 17.)

What selflessness. Death was on the other side of the moon. He was moments away from the agonizing experience— separation from God the Father. Yet the Savior's mind took ease by caring for the emotional and spiritual state of others.

In particular, Simon Peter was on His mind. At one point during the Last Supper, He turned to Peter and said, "Simon, Simon, Satan has asked to sift all of you as wheat. But *I have prayed for you*, Simon, that your faith may not fail. And when you have turned back, strengthen your brothers" (Luke 22:31–32, emphasis added).

Can't you just picture it? I can see Jesus standing in this moment with the quiet authority of a state trooper requesting a speeding motorist's papers. The trooper doesn't raise his voice above a whisper—doesn't go out of his way to intimidate. There's no need. He stands on the driver's side of the car exuding a quiet strength. Standing behind him is the entire state government. He's not standing alone, though he's the only one in sight. The whole government is in support of the trooper as he's discharging his duty.

The trooper's words wield power and authority that demand action. His authority is not dressed with animation, a raised voice, a threatening tone, or a disturbing grimace. Nothing but a quiet command is heard, and nothing but a pleasant demeanor is seen. Yet the speeding driver immediately presents his driver's license, registration, and insurance certificate. The strength of the trooper's authority goes unquestioned.

Similarly Jesus's words to Peter exude a greater confidence. The answer to combat Satan's appeal to attack Peter was met with the words, "I have prayed for you." Jesus's words here highlight the power of prayer. They illuminated the elevated position of prayer. He showcased its importance and value in all kinds of circumstances, even when it comes to combat.

## SATAN'S PLANNED ATTACK

Prior to Jesus's sobering dialogue with Peter, Satan had approached God with a singular appeal. He wanted—and received approval within limits—to "sift [Peter] as wheat." Every first-century individual understood this metaphor. The sifting of wheat was a twofold process. Wheat was placed upon a coarse mesh called a sieve. The first step was to shake the sieve, allowing the grain to fall to the ground or into an awaiting container. The second step was to throw away all of the stones, chaff, and other unwanted debris caught by the sieve. Quite often the sieve was waved in the air to allow the wind to blow away the debris.

Satan's intention was to sift Peter's faith—to shake it up so that he'd fall. The enemy already had Judas. Peter was to be next. Satan's devilish hope was to separate Peter's faith—the desirable parts from the undesirable.

Peter was a major influencer with the other disciples. If he fell, the faith of the others would certainly weaken. That's why the New Testament scholar Norval Geldenhuys writes, "Satan will make a last desperate attempt to break up the circle of Jesus' disciples and to cast out its members like chaff scattered by the wind. Satan desires that in the sifting process 'no wheat shall remain,' but that all (like Judas) will be blown away like chaff."[1]

## JESUS'S PLANNED COUNTERATTACK

Unmoved by Satan's appeal, Jesus's counterattack was simple: *pray*. With a greater sense of quiet authority than any state trooper, Jesus announced to Peter, "I have prayed for you." The matter was settled. Peter's faith would remain intact despite the blow that he'd shortly receive. Prayer would buoy his faith.

Peter was not, however, to treat the matter lightly. Jesus prefaced His warning by repeating Simon's name. What Peter heard was, "Simon, Simon." The repetition was intended to ready Peter for the sobering words that would follow. In this case it was a warning.

This is just like when my wife, Marlinda, calls my whole name—first and last. I brace myself. She commands my undivided attention in that moment. I know she's about to say something that should not be misunderstood or heard partially. When this happens (and it's not too often, thankfully!), some warning or cautionary dialogue will follow.

This is what Jesus was offering to Peter. It was a warning not meant to frighten Peter. Rather, Peter was being called to attention; he needed to be vigilant. Satan had his eyes on Peter and, as usual, was in his devious attack mode. Though Peter was oblivious, Jesus had a surefire solution: prayer. He prayed for Peter.

Since Satan had launched an attack against Peter, there needed to be a more potent counterattack if Peter was to survive. And if anyone knew how to nullify this satanic assault, Jesus did.

This was no ordinary fight. It was a clash with the dark, demonic world. It was designed by Satan—the architect of evil—in a strategic attempt to destroy Peter's present and future influence. The origin of this attack was the spiritual world, which meant the solution must also come from the spiritual world.

Satan's request to sift Peter as wheat is what we nowadays call a *terroristic threat*. Legally speaking, a terroristic threat "is a crime generally involving a threat to commit violence communicated with the intent to terrorize another...to cause serious public inconvenience...[and] may include but is not limited to recklessly endangering another person, harassment, stalking, ethnic intimidation, and criminal mischief."[2] Satan was not just spewing words. He was inviting war with his words.

The only recourse here was to fight using a more powerful weapon. So Jesus went into battle mode. Being the Son of God, He had many weapons to combat Satan's attack. Put aside for a moment His omnipotence, which would have been a surefire way to annihilate any and every adversary. Jesus could also have used angels to fight Satan's threats against Peter. We know this because when He stopped His disciples from using physical force to ward off His arrest in the Garden of Gethsemane, He said, "Do you think I cannot call on my Father, and he will at once put at my disposal more than twelve legions of angels?" (Matt. 26:53). A Roman legion in Jesus's day had roughly 5,400 soldiers. Twelve legions would mean, then, that Jesus could have easily summoned 64,800 angels to fight against Satan!

Furthermore, remember that terroristic threats are intended to harm more than one person. Their aim is to create public or wide-scale mayhem. Satan's aim was to go through Peter to get to *all* of the other disciples. With such a ripple effect tied to Satan's threat, Jesus did not even think twice about an alternative to prayer. Summoning one, two, or twelve legions of angels was not His approach. It was not even necessary. Prayer was enough! It is a more than adequate weapon. It is a most powerful one.

Prayer was Jesus's weapon of choice. It must also become yours.

## WHAT KIND OF WEAPON IS PRAYER?

Weapons are used to protect, defend, and even defeat enemies, and Satan was clearly Jesus's enemy. He was threatening to sabotage one of Jesus's lieutenants—Peter. Yet through prayer Jesus brought His enemy into striking distance. Through prayer Satan was sure to loosen his grip on Peter.

But what kind of weapon is this? Let's take a look.

### It's our key advantage.

In the military there is something known as homeland advantage. No one knows your home, your forest, or your land better than you. If you must fight, try to fight in your own backyard. You know all the good spots—the advantageous high grounds from which you can launch an attack. When you bring your problems into the field of prayer, you declare home-field advantage.

Similarly, in the world of sports we're familiar with this concept of home-field advantage too. The home team gains an upper hand by playing on their familiar field in front of their own fans. My friend's son, Ted, knows this all too well. He's a diehard fan of New York's professional soccer team, the Red Bulls. When Ted was away in graduate school in Delaware, he could not pass up free tickets to see the Red Bulls play the Philadelphia Union team in Philly. It was less than an hour's drive away. Decked in his Red Bulls' regalia, Ted excitedly took his seat in the stands, ready to cheer on his team.

In case you don't know, Philly fans are crazy. They take team support to an all-time high in *all* sports, be it baseball, football, basketball, or soccer. These fans get rowdy and at times—even criminal—to show their team support. To give you an example, let me tell you about the time my youngest daughter, Jessica, called home during her first semester at the University of Pennsylvania, located in the heart of Philadelphia. With incredulity in her voice, she said,

"Dad, the Philadelphia Phillies just won a game. The fans are turning over cars in the city to celebrate. It's scary here, Dad."

Back to Ted's experience at the Red Bulls game in Philly. Moments after he took his seat, ready to root for his beloved team, two police officers walked over to him. With a warm yet firm greeting, they said, "Sir, we would like to escort you to another section to sit. You're sitting in a really rowdy section, surrounded by Union fans. It's not safe for you."

They walked Ted some distance away into a nicer, more expensive seat. This was not to show him any kind of red carpet treatment or their way of offering a new attendee to their stadium some kind of complimentary gesture. Rather, the action was meant to remove Ted from harm's way. His Red Bulls outfit was baiting the Philadelphia Union fans, like waving a red flag in front of a bull. He was sure to draw attention and possibly blows.

The takeaway from this story is: home-field advantage is something fierce. If you are a visiting fan—a stranger to that field—watch out! Apart from your level of discomfort, you will be at a severe disadvantage.

Let's capitalize on this fact by conducting our fights with the enemy on our home field of prayer. This was Jesus's home turf, and it must be ours too. But Satan knows nothing about the field of prayer. To whom can he pray for help? No one! Who are his supportive, encouraging fans—his demons? Perhaps. But they too share his disadvantage in the field of prayer.

We have the exact opposite experience. The field of prayer is our home court. In prayer we sense the enveloping presence of God. In prayer we're encouraged by Jesus to use His name when making requests to God (John 16:24). In prayer the Holy Spirit helps us by "interceding for us with groans that words cannot express" (Rom. 8:26). If this is not home-court advantage, I don't know what is.

Furthermore, Scripture declares, "Therefore, since we are surrounded by such a great cloud of witnesses, let us throw off everything that hinders and the sin that so easily entangles. And let us run with perseverance the race marked out for us" (Heb. 12:1). The saints that have gone on before us testify of the effectiveness of the weapon of prayer. They, along with God, are our adoring fans, and their support bolsters us in our efforts.

### It's our teacher.

For many believers, spiritual warfare and the weapons it calls for are shrouded in mystery. J. H. Jowett, a famed twentieth-century English preacher, wrote:

> It is in the field of prayer that life's critical battles are lost or won. We must conquer all our circumstances there. We must first of all bring them there. We must survey them there. We must master them there. In prayer we bring our spiritual enemies in the Presence of God and we fight them there. Have you tried that? Or have you been satisfied to meet and fight your foes in the open spaces of the world?[3]

Don't be misguided! Prayer is a most powerful weapon that has been given to you. Use it! Use it often! Use it freely!

When Jesus told Peter, "I have prayed for you," He was also saying, "I have brought you and the problems you're about to face into the very presence of God. In prayer I have surveyed your needs. In prayer I have discovered a strategy to thwart the enemy's plans." Jesus then declared that this had been done so that Peter's "faith may not fail." The focal point of Jesus's prayer was the protection of Peter's faith. This means His prayer was concentrated, topical, and strategic.

I can't help but wonder if the strategy to focus in prayer on Peter's faith was actually *discovered* in prayer. Although I cannot confidently make that conclusion from the limited information found in the text, I can, however, say with great confidence that battle strategies are unearthed, discovered, and mined through prayer. Each act of intercession brings more illumination and military wisdom. As you use the weapon of prayer, you get increased battle skill. You will learn what to do and how to do it, and even when to simply be still.

It was into the field of prayer that the apostle Paul also brought his enemy and his problems. And it was in this very field that he gained the wisdom to simply yield to the grace of God, as he says, "Three times I pleaded with the Lord to take it away from me. But he said to me, 'My grace is sufficient for you, for my power is made perfect in weakness'" (2 Cor. 12:8–9).

Why not do the same? Bring your problems, your worries, and the enemy into your prayer closet. Fight them there! Gain strategy there! Get the victory there!

## THE POWER OF PRAYER

Let me tell you a story about the power of prayer. Through prayer, a man named Jimmy experienced a much needed victory for his extended family. He had noticed his family's behavior had become increasingly unhealthy and cultlike. Their church was far more legalistic than he first thought. Their church taught that women were hellbound if they wore pants or lipstick, dyed their hair, or wore jewelry. And if anyone missed a day of church, God forbid, the pastor would call their names from the pulpit. This kind of spiritually abusive leadership made them guilt-ridden and afraid of God.

Jimmy's relatives were adults, but this damaging church culture had produced such a fear in their hearts concerning their pastor that he controlled their lives. The prayer strategy Jimmy chose was to ask God to open their eyes to see and experience the true love of Jesus Christ. When opportunity presented itself, he would lovingly and patiently present certain Bible passages to them that showed what the Father's love is like. The parable of the prodigal son was a big hit. That story showed a patient and loving father even when faced with a sinful son. Jimmy told them that's what God's love is like toward us.

The day finally came when his family bravely announced: "We must leave our church." Jimmy walked them through the need to resign in a godly way as a sign of true courage. Although fear said, "Run away; don't say anything; just quietly go," Jimmy prayed them through to such a point of deliverance and victory that they left the church in honor and not shame.

Today Jimmy's family is actively involved in a Bible-believing church where they are able to enjoy God. What a testimony to the real power of prayer!

## PRAYER IS GOD'S LANGUAGE

Prayer is a conversation with God. Through words, thoughts, and even gestures God hears our request. In fact, He says of His people, "Before they call I will answer; while they are still speaking I will hear" (Isa. 65:24). This is not an isolated passage. In an earlier generation David confidently sang, "When I am in distress, I call to you, because you answer me" (Ps. 86:7). People who have experience with God have a common testimony: God answers prayer! Jeremiah declared, "Then you will call upon me and come and pray to me, and I will listen to you" (Jer. 29:12). Again, throughout human history we learn from many sources that responding to prayer is God's business.

His willingness to answer prayers makes prayer an accessible key to unlocking the door of our problems. God promises that when we pray He listens. This word *listen* in the Hebrew—the original language of the Old Testament scriptures—means "to listen attentively." It also means "to discern, to be content, to give ear with a mind to consent." Not only does God hear our prayers, He also listens attentively with a heart to say *yes*. This makes prayer powerful!

Prayer is also powerful because it is the language God responds to. He invites prayers. He welcomes prayer. He is moved by prayer. He responds to prayer. These assertions are not my opinion. Nor are they some unique interpretation that I found in an obscure passage of Scripture. The truth about prayer and its power is in plain sight.

To illustrate what I mean, let me ask you: Have you ever tried to direct someone, just with words, to find something that is misplaced? I have. It's hard, especially when you are not sure where you last saw the item. One time I was trying to tell Marlinda where I last saw the pair of scissors with the red handle. We always keep them in the same drawer in the kitchen—the one closest to the sink. Somehow on this particular day they were not there.

When she asked, "Honey, have you seen the red scissors?" from the other room, I shouted, "In the living room, I think." I then tried to guide her with words to the exact place in the living room where I thought I saw them. It went something like this: "When you walk in the living room, stop in front of the coffee table, move the lamp to the left about two feet. Then look next to this month's *Runner's World* magazine, and I believe they are there."

After a few minutes I heard her sigh in frustration all the way from my office. Then the words of disappointment followed: "I don't see them!" At that, my clueless response ended the conversation: "I don't know where they are." As life would have it, a week later the scissors were spotted—under a book, hidden, in the living room.

Seeing prayer as a powerful weapon is not like that. There is no need to search for any length of time. It's in plain sight and always in plain sight.

Prayer is God's language. Just as English is the official language in the United States, prayer is the official language of heaven. You don't have to travel far within America to find someone who speaks or understands English. You don't need to locate an interpreter to translate for you. Most Americans understand and speak the language. In fact, you'll find some narrow-minded Americans who believe that you can't be an American unless you know and speak English. I don't believe that. But this illustration clarifies my singular point: prayer is the official language of God. This makes prayer powerful. Because when you're praying, you're speaking God's language. According to Jeremiah God hears and responds when you communicate to Him in this language (Jer. 29:12–14).

Or think about how it is when you *don't* speak the native language of a people group or place. I recently experienced this on a trip to Florence, Italy. A meal at a restaurant brought me face-to-face with the limits of my Italian. I don't speak, read, or understand the language. And as chance would have it, my servers and the few patrons in my vicinity did not know English. I could not express what I was thinking at the moment. I can tell you, though, that I was thinking, "Houston, we have a problem!" I fumbled my way through the menu selection. It wasn't pretty, but I was determined not to leave the restaurant hungry.

This problem can never happen when we pray. Prayer is God's language. You can speak with Him. In fact, He is the one who initiated prayer. He created prayer. He instituted prayer as the vehicle whereby we can speak with Him and even ask Him for help.

Prayer gives you an audience with almighty God. You have direct access into His throne room. As the King of kings, He is able to grant your requests without the need to check in with anyone else. This means that prayer connects you with the ultimate power source—God. Prayer enables you to tie into limitless power.

## WHY IS PRAYER A POWERFUL WEAPON?

A small town in eastern Missouri was stunned last year when prayers miraculously breathed life into a dying woman at the scene of a harrowing accident. A nineteen-year-old college coed, her vital signs dropping, was trapped among the twisted metal of her upside-down vehicle after a deadly highway collision. Tireless attempts to free her from the wreckage by New London, Missouri, fire chief Raymond Reed and his team proved fruitless. *USA Today* reported that Reed, knowing the young woman was running out of time, was about to make the risky decision to flip the car upright although the sudden change in pressure might prove deadly for the victim.

Then out of nowhere, a silver-haired priest stepped forward, approached the car, and began to pray openly with the young woman. Reed says the priest sprinkled oil on him, the young woman, and nearby rescue workers.

Suddenly a team of volunteers appeared from a neighboring town, and roughly twenty men pitched in to turn the mangled car upright. The critically injured victim, whose vital signs dramatically improved, emerged from the car and was rushed to the hospital. She had several broken bones, but the prognosis was good.

"I think it's a miracle," Reed told reporters, adding that he lost the priest in the crowd, never to see him again.[4]

Prayer has power. That's why the weapon of prayer is so damaging to the plans of the enemy. The source of this power is not in us or in our level of spirituality. The source is two-fold. First, we have been given authority to use prayer as a weapon. Second, we've been instructed that when we pray, we must pray in faith.

Heaven responds to faith-laced prayers. Faith is a badge that proves our God-given authority when we unleash the weapon of prayer. Leonard Ravenhill, in his book *Revival Praying*, writes, "Faith is the muscle by which we lift the load; faith is the currency by which we make purchases in the spiritual kingdom; faith is spiritual sight."[5]

**It gives us authority.**

The power source is directly associated with the authority we have been given to use Jesus's name. He said, "Until now you have not asked for anything in my name. Ask and you will receive, and your joy will be complete" (John 16:24).

Jesus gave us the authority to use His name when we approach God. We have the legal right to use the weapon of prayer when we fight. Think back to the state trooper pulling over the motorist. The guy in the crisp uniform does not hold authority in and of himself. Power does not originate or lie within him. His power has nothing to do with his imposing physical stature. A strong personality doesn't even come into play. The genesis of his authority lies solely in the fact that he has been sent by the state to act on behalf of the state in which he serves.

Similarly our authority to wield the weapon of prayer lies squarely in the authority given to us by Jesus. He's the crowning monarch who has the legal and jurisdictional right to grant such authority for servants in His state—the kingdom of God. Paul's confidence in praying three times stemmed from knowledge of his authority to pray. He was assured that God would respond and give him the answers—the battle strategy—he sought. We have the same right, the same authority, to ask with an expectation to receive.

A. B. Simpson, founder of the Christian and Missionary Alliance denomination, was a great man of prayer. Through prayer he discovered this secret:

> Probably this is the best rule about prayer: to pray until we understand the mind of the Lord about it, and get sufficient light, direction, and comfort to satisfy our hearts.... As soon as the assurance comes, we should stop praying, and henceforth everything should be praise.[6]

If your mind is now wondering about things you've stopped praying for because of discouragement or some other reason, put the book down. Take a few minutes right now and bend your knees in prayer. Resurrect the issue with God and see what He wants to do about it. You do not have the luxury of silencing your voice in God's throne room. Pray!

**It demonstrates our faith.**

A few years ago I watched the HBO program *Real Sports With Bryant Gumbel*, where Nik Wallenda of the Flying Wallenda family was being interviewed. This is the guy who in June 2013 walked fifteen hundred feet on a two-inch-thick cable a quarter mile above the Little Colorado River Gorge near the Grand Canyon. It took him twenty-two minutes to walk across with no harness or safety net while winds up to thirty miles per hour whipped around him and the wire swayed.[7]

"Thank You, Lord. Thank You for calming that cable, God," he said about thirteen minutes into his walk.[8]

He told Gumbel in the interview, "The most important thing when walking across a tight wire while curling the forty-six-pound bar is balance, focus, and attention.

"When I was younger and I'd be walking the wire, someone would hit me from the side and it would be a pinecone or a football would go in front of my face. Or you never knew what was coming at you. It was my parents trying to distract me so I'd be prepared for anything. Often they would come up behind me and shake the wire; I wouldn't expect it. We'd try to train for all of that so that we're always focused on that cable."[9]

You better believe Nik's prayer was steeped in faith. His life depended on God hearing—and answering—him.

But even if the subject of our prayers is not a life-and-death matter, the need for faith still exits. The principle is explained in this and other passages: "And without faith it is impossible to please God, because anyone who comes to him must believe that he exists and that he rewards those who earnestly seek him" (Heb. 11:6). God is constrained to respond to faith. Faith gets His attention. It moves Him.

Conversely, doubt is the opposite of faith, so it has opposite effect with God. God is unresponsive where there is doubt. Doubt cannot secure His attention. Doubt cannot move God. The impact of this negative rule is shared in the practical letter that James wrote:

> If any of you lacks wisdom, you should ask God, who gives generously to all without finding fault, and it will be given to you. But when you ask, you must believe and not doubt, because the one who doubts is like a wave of the sea, blown and tossed by the wind. That person should not expect to receive anything from the Lord. Such a person is double-minded and unstable in all they do.
>
> —JAMES 1:5–8

Since prayers asked in faith connect us to God, our prayer connects us to the ultimate power source. The omnipotent, limitless power of God becomes accessible to us when we pray. The caveat, however, is that prayer is meaningless without faith. We cannot afford to step onto the battlefield with doubt in our hearts. God's fighters must clothe themselves in faith. Faith activates the weapon of prayer!

To illustrate this point further, I'll close by sharing this story:

There was a farmer who had three sons: Jim, John, and Sam. No one in the family ever attended church or had time for God. The pastor and the others in the church tried for years to interest the family in the things of God to no avail. Then one day Sam was bitten by a rattle-snake. The doctor was called, and he did all he could to help Sam, but Sam's prognosis was very dim indeed. So the pastor was called in. The pastor arrived, and began to pray as follows:

"Almighty God, we thank You that in Your wisdom You sent this rattlesnake to bite Sam. He has never been inside the church and it's doubtful that he has ever prayed or even acknowledged Your existence. Now we trust that this experience will be a valuable lesson to him and will lead to his genuine repentance.

"And now, O Lord, please send another rattlesnake to bite Jim, and another to bite John, and another really big one to bite the old man. God, the only thing that will do this family any real good is rattlesnakes; so, Lord, send us bigger and better rattlesnakes. Amen.[10]

Even in this comical story the power of prayer can be seen. It is one powerful weapon. Use it in your battles!

*Chapter 3*

# OUR GOD IS A GENERAL

For all her life, my youngest daughter, Jessica, has been a PK—a pastor's kid. I remember one time when she was about five, she had a chance to sit in the main sanctuary with the adults for the first time. It was a very big deal because little ones routinely spent the entire service in children's church.

Jess knew on some level that her dad was a pastor. But somehow her five-year-old mind couldn't wrap itself around the full scope of what that meant. To her, I was the guy who read bedtime stories, played hide-and-seek, and let her and her sister pummel me during snowball fights. You know—the things dads do.

That particular morning, after the worship singers took their seats, I got up from the pew and began to walk toward the platform. Alarmed by what she perceived to be a punishable act, Jess jumped out of her seat and whispered loudly. "Get down from there, Daddy! Get down before you get into trouble!"

It was so cute.

But when you think about it, it makes sense she responded that way. Jess knew me as her dad, a caregiver. She simply could not see me beyond that role. So she was protecting me—or so she thought. In reality she had confined me to one very narrow lane: daddy.

Sometimes I wonder if we are doing the same to God. I mean, we see God in a limited way because of the divine titles and names we are most familiar with. Titles create expectation. They provide a framework by which we see someone, interact with them, and come to expect them to relate to us. Scripture presents dozens of titles and names for God. Each one gives a view of God and an expectation of how God will relate to us. And I'm willing to bet there are more than a few titles for God that most influence the way you relate to Him.

## OUR COMFORTABLE NAMES FOR GOD

Let's take a look at some of the most popular titles and names for God and then see how those might skew our view of Him in a narrow direction.

First up, in the Old Testament we see David say, "The LORD is my shepherd" (Ps. 23:1). In another psalm Asaph sings, "Hear us, Shepherd of Israel" (Ps. 80:1). The shepherd title for God was part of a national song. It was not an unfamiliar title for God in Israel. These two psalmists didn't arbitrarily choose to pin the vocation of shepherd on God. The Lord used that noun to describe Himself. Just as a natural shepherd cares for, guides, and protects his sheep from predators, so the Lord performs those duties for us.

We also see God called "Wonderful Counselor" (Isa. 9:6). This compound name gives us a different picture of God than the shepherd title does. Here, we see that the work of salvation and the redemption of humanity did not require God to seek the counsel, advice, or wisdom of another. He was able to reach back into time and reach forward into the future to carve out an infallible plan of redemption. God is the supreme fountainhead of wisdom and planning! His very name declares that fact. This knowledge of God helps us to relate to Him as the all-knowing, wise God.

In that same verse in Isaiah we are given the chance to look through the lens of another compound name for God,

"Everlasting Father," to learn a third way of relating to God. From this title we understand God has a loving, paternal concern for everyone who commits themselves to His care. This divine name brings us into a deeper feeling of security while at the same time creating an expectation for God to nurture, train, and develop us into sons and daughters. This expectation is not short-term, either. God places a permanent responsibility on His own shoulders by attaching the word *everlasting* to the title.

Also in the Old Testament we find Jeremiah teaching us that God is a potter. The passage says, "'Can I not do with you, Israel, as this potter does?' declares the LORD. 'Like clay in the hand of the potter, so are you in my hand, Israel'" (Jer. 18:6). From this passage we have God's approval to pray to Him—the potter—to be shaped and molded by His hands into a beautiful masterpiece.

When we turn to the New Testament, we are exposed to even more dimensions of God through other titles and names given to Him. Jesus said, "I am the true vine, and my Father is the gardener" (John 15:1). In His capacity as gardener, we learn that God prunes our lives by cutting away dead branches so we can become more fruitful. This metaphor allows us to focus our prayers Godward for His pruning.

In Romans 15:13 we learn that God is a God of hope. From this title, Paul outlines what our expectation of God can be. He wrote, "May the God of hope fill you with all joy and peace as you trust in him, so that you may overflow with hope by the power of the Holy Spirit." If you're facing a bleak situation, in faith you can pray to the God of hope and discover Him giving you so much hope that you'll actually have excess.

God is a God of comfort too. Paul points out, "Praise be to the God and Father of our Lord Jesus Christ, the Father of compassion and the God of all comfort, who comforts us in all our troubles, so that we can comfort those in any trouble with the comfort we ourselves receive from God" (2 Cor. 1:3–4). The value of being comforted, consoled, or soothed is not fully appreciated until you are distraught and disheartened. At such low points the ability to seek God for comfort in and of itself is comforting to know. Our God is not unfeeling or unsympathetic of our emotional needs. He cares enough to offer us the strength of His comfort. You can approach Him with that understanding whenever you're feeling blue or down.

All of these titles and names for God are great. They're legitimate. God presents Himself to us in these ways. But we need to be aware that there's more to God than these kindly titles. There's more to God than the tender and protective ways He relates to us. Just look at what we learn in Hebrews 12—that God is a consuming fire (v. 29)! This suggests God is not to be dealt with casually, carelessly, or with an attitude of familiarity. In fact, the passage in Hebrews says we're to "be thankful, and so worship God acceptably with reverence and awe" (v. 28). Now, the wrath of God is not a very popular topic. We're so convinced of our spiritual rights that we demand God treat us in certain ways. Even so, God is still a consuming fire. None of our desiring Him to be different can change that. He demands our reverence and awe!

## BROADEN YOUR PERSPECTIVE

So to make room for new understandings about God, we need to broaden our perspective. By way of example, perhaps you remember the recent story of the father who wanted to broaden the perspective of his teenage daughter. I was shocked alongside many other Americans who tuned in to the *Good Morning America* news story to see a fifty-two-year-old man wearing a pair of short shorts—the kind Daisy Duke wore in the old sitcom *The Dukes of Hazzard*. They were tight, short, revealing, and embarrassing, to say the least.

This dad was tired of having his nineteen-year-old daughter, Myley, ignore his paternal advice to dress modestly. She, like so many other teenage girls, favored skimpy clothes to show off her curves. In her effort to look "hot" she found nothing wrong with the long seductive stares she drew from guys who undressed her with their eyes.

Myley hadn't been buying her dad's lessons on how modesty safeguards her worth as a young lady. So he used a different method to convey the same truth. He came out of character. He was no longer the conservative, modest father who dressed his age. Instead, he cut off the legs of a pair of old jeans and turned them into his own Daisy Duke shorts. The entire family was shocked, embarrassed, and speechless.

He even kept them on when they played miniature golf at the public course. Strangers pointed, stared, and snickered, as did his daughter. And then, to get an even bigger laugh, she posted a picture of him wearing his short shorts on one of her social media sites. To her surprise, the photo went viral. Overnight it received more than 130,000 comments, drawing the attention of media outlets, which led to *Good Morning America* requesting an interview with the family.

Ironically the dad's behavior made a lasting impression on Myley. Her takeaway, when asked by the reporter, was to say she'd learned her lesson. "It got the point across," she said.[1]

The sentiment beneath Myley's response to the reporter is what I latched on to. Through the experience she got a fresh perspective of her dad, which caused her to understand a larger truth he needed her to know but that she'd been immune to learning prior to this experience.

This is what God does for us!

# THE AWE OF GOD

Unlike Myley's dad, our heavenly Father doesn't need to act out of character to get our attention. However, all the greater truths He would have us know about Himself are listed right there in Scripture—one of which is the truth of God being a general and our being drafted into His army.

To explore the truth of this title for God and how it impacts us, let's revisit that earlier passage regarding God's identity as a consuming fire. Did you catch the mention of the word *awe* in that passage (Heb. 12:28–29)? It's an essential component to what we're going to learn about relating to God as a general. And it's a truth about God that runs throughout the Scriptures.

For instance, during a moment of disappointment with Israel, recounted in the Book of Jeremiah, God says to Israel, "Consider then and realize how evil and bitter it is for you when you forsake the LORD your God and *have no awe of me*" (Jer. 2:19, emphasis added). This word *awe* captures the idea of being so utterly shaken by what you see, feel, or come into contact with that you're left speechless, startled, and sometimes afraid. When some people experience awe, they quiver or fall out, physically collapsing, because they are so overcome with emotions of fascination.

Perhaps you have experienced something of this when encountering one of the many wonders of the world, such as the Grand Canyon, Niagara Falls, or Mount Everest. What about the experience of witnessing a baby take his first step or say her first word, or a deaf person hearing music for the first time? The feeling of awe hits us in these moments.

I experienced it a few years ago when Marlinda and I had the privilege of visiting Niagara Falls. We had both seen the falls as children, but this time it was different. To see up front this majestic waterfall that had been around since the beginning of time was mind numbing. The mist sprinkled on us as we stared from the safety of the nearby platform. We were in awe.

Our hotel room offered a direct view of the falls. Each day I woke up and stared at them almost in a hypnotic trance. I had my morning devotions and coffee at the desk while gazing at them. Then on one particular morning I happened to study a wall hanging that showed people gathered around the falls in the late 1800s. As my eyes moved from section to section, I was amazed at the fact that the waters were still pouring over the falls today, just as in the image on the wall.

In that moment the Holy Spirit interrupted my inspection of the artwork with these words: "David, the same way the water never stops flowing over the falls is the same way My love will never stop flowing over you." At that I was undone. My awe of God was brought to an all-time high. I was awe-struck by God like a kid who just received a high-five from his favorite pro ball player.

Having a sense of awe about God is important not only to God but also to us. It feeds our expectation of Him. It drives our prayer life. It fuels our excitement about God. To stir the interest of Israel toward spiritual things and turn their hearts back to Him, God reminds them of His promise to restore the city of Judah. He excitedly declared: "Then this city will bring me renown, joy, praise and honor before all nations on earth that hear of all the good things I do for it; and *they will be in awe* and will tremble at the abundant prosperity and peace I provide for it" (Jer. 33:9, emphasis added). Here again we see God's fascination with the emotion of awe. Awe keeps the relationship fresh and thrilling. Without it, we lumber about without a sense of enthusiasm.

God is not the only one who recognizes the value of awe. Stanford University researchers recently tried to unearth the value and its benefits through a study, which concluded that those who experienced awe:

- Had more time available and were less impatient

- Were more willing to volunteer their time to help others

- More strongly preferred experiences over material products

- Experienced a greater boost in life satisfaction[2]

Could it be that God wants to use the power of awe to catapult you into holy moments where you are more patient, apt to lend a helping hand to others, less materialistic, and enjoying a greater satisfaction in life? I think so. Apart from these academic findings, imagine the spiritual benefits associated with holding God in awe.

Drs. Will and Charles Mayo, brothers and founders of the world famous Mayo Clinics, make an additional link between science and faith. Speaking of their human limitations and dependence on God, Dr. Will Mayo said, "I have seen patients that were dead by all standards. We knew they could not live. But I have seen a minister come to the bedside and do something for him that I could not do, although I have done everything in my professional power. But something touched some immortal spark in him and in defiance of medical knowledge and materialistic common sense, that patient LIVED!"[3] Awe makes even scientists humbled with silence when God does things that baffle all reason.

All of which is to say, you cannot allow Satan to harden your heart toward God. The heart is the dwelling place of awe—the foundation of our intimacy with God. Awe cannot be left vulnerable, unprotected, or prone to depletion of its power. Hardness of spiritual heart occurs over time, slowly and steadily, just like the hardening of the arteries in the physical heart. The Puritan writer John Owen says, "There is nothing more grievous to the Lord, nothing that serves the purposes of Satan more... [than hardness toward God]. Satan rejoices when he can fill your heart with such hard thoughts of God. Satan's purpose from the beginning was to fill mankind with lies about God."[4]

Lies about God are not just untruths about His nature, essence, and personality. We get that. Even a cursory reading of Scripture will open our eyes to the real character of God. Many believers easily avoid becoming prey to those kinds of lies because the benevolent nature of God is so visible. However, there is another kind of lie—a more insidious one. This kind lets us see only a limited glimpse of God. This kind makes us stop searching, growing, and yearning for more of God. Satan's lies can also include the depiction of God as limited and one-sided.

The many titles and names of God should not limit us to a one-dimensional knowledge and view of God. Rather, it should awaken in us a thirst to really know God. This is what A. W. Tozer called for in his classic work *The Pursuit of God* when he wrote, "Moses used the fact that he knew God as an argument for knowing Him better."[5] Moses demonstrated that the more you know God, the more you crave to know God. Awe keeps you awestruck.

Ultimately what I'm leading you to see here is that if we see God only as a doting father, a humble shepherd, or a gardener, we unwittingly miss out on the fact that He's a mighty general too—the commander of the army of the Lord, in fact. Let's turn our attention to this truth about God now.

## OUR GENERAL, GOD

To begin, let's acknowledge that not everyone in an army gets a chance to meet the general. He's too important, too busy, too far removed from the regular rank and file, too engaged in weighty matters. But unlike earthly generals, God gives each of us access to Him regardless of our rank. This privilege alone must keep us in a constant state of awe!

Also unlike earthly generals, God is the perfect general. His military strategies are impeccable. His orders are flawless. His treatment of His army is over the top. Though God is leading an army during wartime—spiritual wartime—His troops are still driven and maintained by principles of love, honor, mutual respect, and value of human life and dignity.

To have accomplished such a feat throughout every human era is yet another reason to hold God in a state of awe.

To learn more about God the General, let's look at the story of Joshua. As he prepared to launch an attack against the army of Jericho, he had to stop dead in his tracks. He had what the scholars call a *theophany*—an appearance of God in human form. Standing in front of Joshua was a man with a drawn sword, to whom Joshua bravely asked the question, "Are you for us or for our enemies?" (Josh. 5:13). The answer he received moved him to assume the posture of submission and humility: "'Neither,' he replied, 'but as commander of the army of the LORD I have now come.' Then Joshua fell facedown to the ground in reverence, and asked him, 'What message does my Lord have for his servant?'" (v. 14).

Once Joshua became aware of the presence of the general—God—near him, he assumed the position of obedience. Not only that, but he also asked for orders. That's because generals give orders! Soldiers cannot be victorious without orders from their commanding officers.

This is precisely why prayer must become a two-way activity. We know we have an obligation and responsibility to pray—to make a request of God. But equally important, if not more so, is our responsibility to listen for God's orders and directives in return. Imagine how much better the outcome of our battles would be if we did this. Instead of scurrying out of His presence without a clue as to what to do, where to go, or how to accomplish the task before us—assuming we even know what our task is—we would patiently wait to hear from our general and then follow what He tells us to do.

To give you an example of what I mean, let me tell you the story of a young woman named Grace. For as long as she could remember, Grace wanted to be a teacher. She loved learning, and she loved seeing how knowledge sparked light in a child's eyes. But getting ahead in her chosen field would mean an advanced degree, and Grace knew her limited funds could pose a challenge.

After she completed her undergraduate studies, she began praying. She researched various master's programs in the field of education. She had no money; still, her faith in God pushed her forward. She was sure her career choice was much more than a vocation. It was God's call on her life—a way for her to help others.

She came across the master's program in education leadership offered at Oral Roberts University (ORU) and immediately knew it was for her. Before she began to fill out the application, she prayed. While she completed the application, Grace prayed more. And just before she mailed in the application, her prayers continued.

Not only was Grace accepted to the program, but also to her amazement, without any special application or inquiry, she was awarded a graduate assistance package along with a work-study plan. She'd won a full ride to ORU's three-year degree program!

During her final semester, however, an unexpected tuition bill of $2,500 was presented to her. Grace again faced the challenge in prayer. One particular day as she prayed, she sat quietly in her dorm listening for the Lord. Out of nowhere came this thought: "Ask Uncle Egbert to pay the tuition balance."

It was unmistakable, yet Grace struggled for a while because her uncle was very tight-fisted when it came to money. Truth be told, he had selective hearing when it came to the subject. Grace shared with me, "Any request we made to Uncle E for money, he would act like he never heard us."

Grace became confident in this plan, however, because she felt the Lord spoke to her. Armed with that word, she approached her uncle. And true to form, the phone went silent the moment she asked him if he would consider paying the $2,500 balance of her tuition. He changed the topic, never answering Grace.

But she kept praying that God would soften her uncle's heart. Sure enough, a couple weeks later, an envelope arrived unexpectedly from him. No prompting. No phone call. No heads up. The envelope contained the $2,500 that Grace had requested.

Listening prayer was the reason Grace held a zero balance on graduation day.

We learn from Grace's story that our responsibility as foot soldiers in the army of the Lord is to live in submission to our general. We must always listen to Him and listen for Him. He knows best. He deserves respect—our *full* respect. God, the general, has our best intentions at heart. Our victory is His victory. His victory is our victory. We're on the same side in the same army, serving the same high and noble purpose.

To live in total submission to our general, then, we must not succumb to a conflict of perspectives. Yes, God is a Father. And yes, He will always be our heavenly Father. But to effectively wield the weapon of prayer, you must engage with God the General and not God the Father. God the Father reveals a paternal side, a soft side, a nurturing side. God the General is all business. His focus is on winning a battle, destroying an enemy, and keeping His soldiers in fighting shape.

In my early twenties I worked as an environmental engineer for a consulting firm that had a hard rule that can be instructive to us on this point. They didn't employ spouses. They discovered, as so many other employers have, that husbands and wives tend to see each other through a one-dimensional lens when working together. A business can seldom succeed when family dynamics and "home life" relationships are brought into the workplace. Couples would often struggle to leave their view of their spouses at home. At work the guy is a civil engineer. At home, he's sweetheart, hubby—the love of your life. The roles cannot become confused because the confusion will adversely affect his performance and the office culture. In some instances the wife is the senior person on the job. If she barks out an order to her husband, he may get bent out of shape because his wife is his commanding officer, and his male ego can't handle that.

Although the situation is not quite the same when it comes to the kingdom lifestyle, there is an element that carries over. Many mistakenly get stuck on the fatherhood of God, which creates a certain view and a companion expectation of God. They want to be coddled and hugged and receive copious doses of mercy and ongoing grace regardless of their behavior or performance. This lopsided view of God ignores the fact that God the General is running an army in the middle of a war—a spiritual war. Like any other general, God the General wants to win the battle. There's too much at stake. The battle has been going on since the fall of Satan. He started this battle due to his rebellion. And God is not going to lose out to a rebellious fallen angel. Remember, this is an angel that God created to please Him (Ezek. 28:11–15)!

What kind of signal would it send to the rest of creation if God lost out to Satan? Can you imagine the headline of the heavenly gazette—"Rebellion Pays Off." Ludicrous! It will never happen. God is too brilliant, too focused, too strategic, and too tough to let Satan win. This means that His soldiers must take on the same mind-set as their General.

## CRUISE SHIP OR BATTLESHIP?

To this effect, every soldier in the army of God must ask himself: "Are we on a cruise ship or a battleship here?" The way we answer the question makes a difference in how we carry ourselves, live our lives, and execute our duties. Cruise-ship Christianity is akin to one long vacation. It's like living inside the reality of *The Love Boat*, the popular TV series of the late 1970s, where every day was a party. The passengers boarded to sit back, relax, get comfortable, and demand service. Everyone on the ship was there for a good time. Their goal was to see the sights, enjoy the fun destinations, and return home with souvenirs that remind them of how much fun they had.

The traveler's mind-set and behavior on such a cruise ship is one characterized by laziness. In fact, it almost seems as if there is a competition to see who can be the laziest passenger. I remember hearing a story of a contest hosted many years ago. This multimillionaire wanted to reward the laziest man in America with one million dollars. The wealthy man looked high and low, advertising online and on television commercials. He spared nothing to get the word out. After a few months he found the winner. The guy was actually laying on a beach in New Jersey. The noonday sun was scorching his skin. It was peeling, turning red, and he was dangerously approaching sun stroke level. The millionaire asked him if he knew anything about the contest. The man did not. So the wealthy man filled him in. He concluded that this man was the contest winner. He was the laziest man in America. The million dollar reward was his.

The millionaire said, "Before I give you the money, can you answer this question?"

"Sure," said the lazy man.

"Why are you laying out here in such scorching heat with your skin peeling and all?"

The reply was shocking. "When I first came out here, the sun wasn't up, and I'm not moving!" the lazy man snapped.

"Well, you are the winner of my contest," shared the rich man. "Here is the money."

"Roll me over and put it in my pocket; roll me over and put it in my pocket," the lazy man shamelessly cried.

This is the attitude of cruise-ship Christianity. We are simply lazy! We have a tourist mentality to Christianity. We view the kingdom of God as a cruise ship designed to cater to our every need. This attitude results in a weak church that produces weak Christians. In cruise-ship Christianity there is a lot of complaining but little action. We don't like how things are, but we don't have the courage to fight for change.

Throughout every generation we must fight against the formation and growth of cruise-ship Christianity. And during the days of the American Revolution one pastor did just that. He shocked his congregation out of their deep slumber. As the story goes:

> Though Peter Muhlenberg had preached regularly for the cause of the American colonists, he decided that, in his last sermon, he would have to do something unusual to drive home his point....

After reading from Ecclesiastes 3:1, he said, "There is a time to preach and a time to pray, but there is a time to fight, and that time has now come." Muhlenberg threw off his [clergy] robes to reveal the uniform of a militia colonel.

He then recruited the men of his congregation, who became known as the "German Regiment," which Muhlenberg commanded throughout the war.[6]

I guess a picture is worth a thousand words! Removing the clergy robe to display his army uniform removed the ambiguity. The pastor's message hit home: the kingdom of God is a battleship and not a cruise ship! Those who come on board the battleship are ready for war. They know there are promises worth fighting for, destinations worth securing, and enemies worth conquering.

The battleship mentality deeply respects the General's authority and intent for the expansion of the kingdom, deliverance for the captives, and salvation for the lost. Everything is done with this missional objective. There is not a lot of idle chatter, no complaining about the food or the General. The soldiers are battle ready. They are all aware of the high stakes and their role in the war. The battle cannot be jeopardized on their watch. So they stay focused and ready to change course anytime the God the General gives an order.

You now need to answer the question on a personal level. Are you on a cruise ship or a battleship? The answer is found in your view of God. Among His many roles, He is a General. Let's not forget that!

Chapter 4

# LIFT UP A WAR CRY

For Phyllis and her husband, Ted, their nice drive into New York City from New Jersey on this particular day had become a nightmare. Suddenly they were staring death in the face. Like a science fiction movie, heavy rains and forceful winds came almost out of nowhere. A tornado was headed in their direction at an amazing speed. As their car approached the intersection, a few blocks away they could see the wind gusts splitting trees like a lumberjack chopping firewood. The tornado cut down those huge trees so effortlessly, as if they were toothpicks. It was headed directly toward them, and there was nowhere to turn.

"Jesus, mercy; Jesus, mercy!" Phyllis cried.

It seemed surreal, she later shared. The tornado knocked down a tree about ten feet in front of them. Then all of a sudden it stopped as quickly as it had appeared. The speechless couple offered thanks to God. Once they were home safely, Phyllis fired off an e-mail to our church, where they attend, expressing thanks for teaching her how to pray in all kinds of circumstances.

## PRAYER IS A WAR CRY

Prayer is God's invitation into our battles. Phyllis and Ted didn't have any time to craft some nice ecclesiastical prayer filled with "Thees" and "Thous" based on their circumstance. There was no time. They lifted up a war cry! It was a cry summoning God to the scene. It was a cry of emergency. Only heaven could make a difference in the outcome.

A war cry is a distressing plea. From a military perspective, a war cry is an urgent call made to rally soldiers for battle.

But this method of stirring soldiers is not limited to natural wars or earthly soldiers. Kneeling warriors use it. God uses it! We're told, "The LORD will march out like a champion, like a warrior he will stir up his zeal; with a shout he will raise *the battle cry* and will triumph over his enemies" (Isa. 42:13, emphasis added). Isaiah lets us know that God views Himself as a champion and a warrior, so we have license to see Him that way too.

When champion athletes prepare for the big game, even though their bodies are in great physical shape, they understand the need to get their head in the game. Their minds also affect their performance and the outcome of the match. These champions need to be in a certain head space until the match ends.

I have close knowledge of this reality from the privilege I've been given to lead a number of chapel services for the New York Giants and Jets. When I'm asked to lead a Bible study on Saturday night—the night before the big game—I recognize that my role is to help these big guys stay focused.

One time I brought one of the men from my congregation along. I thought, "A football fan and a godly man—this will be great." But when I arrived at the hotel, I was told that only I could enter the meeting room. My travel companion had to remain in the hotel's lobby—coach's orders.

I quickly understood that the coach was safeguarding his champions. He didn't want some doting fan asking for autographs, commenting on a player's past performance, or engaging in any type of conversation that would pose a mental distraction to the event at hand—Sunday's big game.

God feels the same way, if not more. Not only does He refer to Himself as a champion, but He also adds *warrior* to the description. And as a warrior does, God stirs up His zeal. He psyches Himself up for battle. God rouses the emotion and mental picture that will draw the best out of Him in the battle. God is always at peak performance. He's omnipotent! There is never a time that we'll catch Him napping or functioning below "God standard," if there is such a thing.

I understand that I'm using human terms to describe God's behavior here, which might seem like faulty theology. But sometimes for the sake of understanding, it's important to use human terms that we mortal beings can comprehend. Isaiah was inspired by the Holy Spirit to use these human terms so that we would form a good mental picture of the merciful nature of God to prepare Himself to go to battle on our behalf.

Again, prayer is a type of war cry. It's one of the ways we use prayer as a weapon. And the cry serves two functions. First, it lets the enemy know we know what he's up to—that we recognize his encroachment on our turf. Second, it wakes up the sleeping soldiers on our side. It brings everyone to attention; they're fully alert and vigilant. Spiritual warriors immediately transition from lukewarmness of heart and inattentiveness of mind to a weapon-toting state of vigilance.

Regular war cries are needed in the church to keep us in battle-ready mode. Oftentimes it takes crisis before the war cry can be sounded. And it certainly takes a huge crisis for the war cry to be heeded once sounded.

## LEARN FROM MORDECAI'S EXAMPLE

Reading the Old Testament can be disheartening when you come across the huge blocks of time where Israel languished spiritually. God's chosen people lived long periods of time in a state of apostasy. Their prayerlessness gave way to spiritual lives with many ebbs and flows. It took impassioned spiritual warriors to sound the war cry and call the nation back to intimacy with God.

In the Book of Esther we see this happen. We learn of a Jewish man by the name of Mordecai who lifted up a war cry when the Jews throughout Babylon were facing annihilation. Driven by hatred, Haman, one of the leading nobles to King Xerxes, became indignant because Mordecai did not show him honor. Mordecai—a foreigner to that land—did not bow to pay honor to Haman, though all the other royal officials did whenever they saw him. As a Jew, Mordecai considered it blasphemous to pay Haman the kind of honor he demanded. So Haman plotted and schemed to find a way to destroy this servant of the Lord. Finally the thought came to him: "Why not arrange for all of the Jews throughout Babylon to be killed instead of just Mordecai?"

Armed with his wicked idea, Haman manipulated King Xerxes to pass an unretractable law that allowed the Babylonian citizens to destroy all the Jews on a certain day. This law gave the Babylonians leeway to also plunder the goods of the Jews. To stoke the emotions of the king, Haman promised to contribute a huge sum of money into the national treasury. (See Esther 3:8–9.) The stage was set for a massacre.

**Signal danger with your cry.**

Once Mordecai got wind of the published law sparked by Haman's hatred, he went into immediate action. He sounded the alarm. The Scripture says:

He tore his clothes, put on sackcloth and ashes, and went out into the city, wailing loudly and bitterly. But he went only as far as the king's gate, because no one clothed in sackcloth was allowed to enter it. In every province to which the edict and order of the king came, there was great mourning among the Jews, with fasting, weeping and wailing. Many lay in sackcloth and ashes.

—ESTHER 4:1–3

Upon hearing the news of Haman's plans, Mordecai sobered spiritually. The gravity of the situation drove him to sound a spiritual alarm. He tore his clothes, depicting a torn heart. He was in mourning because of the threat of death and annihilation for all the Jews. Mordecai then clothed himself with sackcloth and ashes. Sackcloth fabric is similar to modern-day burlap. It irritates the skin. Ashes symbolized death and mourning.

Mordecai was in battle mode. He was covered from head to toe with the soldier's uniform. Natural warriors dressed for battle by putting on their shield, breastplate, helmet, sword, shin guards, and other military vestments. Not this warrior. He was a spiritual warrior—a kneeling warrior. His vestments were different. He sounded an alarm, dressed for battle with sackcloth and ashes, and then prayed and fasted.

**Signal others with your cry.**

Mordecai needed to get ahold of God. He needed to rouse the other warriors to prayer. He needed to remind them of the truth Clement of Alexandria hammered home in his day: "Prayer is keeping company with God."[1] Though prayerlessness and spiritual lethargy had taken over the people of God, surely they would hear his war cry and join him in the battle.

So Mordecai did not let up. He wailed loudly and bitterly in the city center. This behavior drew attention. People entering and exiting the palace knew something was wrong. Something unjust was afoot. Foreign diplomats carried the news of this spectacle to their countries. Mordecai was seeking help from every corner of the known world. His thinking was that good people hate evil. They hate injustice. And the master plan to wipe out the Jews living in Babylon had to be stopped. It was unfounded. It was built on hatred. It was an act of injustice. It was inhumane. So he wailed and cried aloud, dressed in sackcloth and ashes, to tell everyone about it.

From the dignitaries to the ordinary rank and file, everyone visiting the city center knew of Mordecai. He became the talk of the town. The maids and eunuchs who worked or lived in the palace started talking about this spectacle. His behavior became a news story. It was unavoidable.

Mordecai's behavior even created annoyance. It said to businesspeople, "Stop focusing on money and commerce and pay attention to the urgent matter at hand." The ghastly sight of Mordecai and his wails that punctuated the streets said to parents, "Stop fussing with your kids and over your kids. Pay attention to the true parental concerns! Your kids' lives are at stake if this law is acted upon." The sound of his cry was an alarm to the careless. It said, "Stop hustling your way through life. Something serious is about to occur. Pay attention! Join me in seeking God's help!" The purpose of Mordecai's war cry was to tell the unmarried Jews in Babylon, "Stop being consumed with the thought of finding the right mate. You can't think about marriage at a time like this. Our lives, destinies, and legacies are at risk. Turn Godward as I have done!" The wailing said to the victimized, "Stop walking around blaming others for your limited life—the good parts of your life that have been taken away by ungodly people. In a short while you'll really be a victim. Call on God! Rouse the heavenly Warrior!"

Can you imagine the ways children processed the wails, cries, and sight of the old man? Mordecai's disturbing behavior did not leave anyone out. The alarm moved even young Jews to prayer. Their childish behavior most likely ceased. Something awful was about to happen to adults *and* children alike. They were not exempt from the need to respond favorably to the war cry. Certainly God would hear the plea of children as they cried to Him for help for their lives.

**Demand strong action with your cry.**

Mordecai's war cry triggered a season of fasting. Other Jews joined him. Still other Jews, independent of him, began to fast for God's help. Fasting is a critical tool in the realm of spiritual warfare. It fuels our prayers for breakthrough.

Fasting is a spiritual act that says to God, "We need Your help more than we need food." Fasting with integrity humbles us. It produces an increased sensitivity to God's will and preferred behavior. Our behavior toward God and others changes. We are more apt to live as true disciples of Jesus Christ rather than worldly people who have a religious bent. In response to our fasting God loosens "the chains of injustice and [unties] the cords of the yoke" (Isa. 58:6). The result of fasting is freedom and breakthrough for the oppressed.

My entrance into the breakthrough power of fasting came thirty years ago. I was working as an environmental engineer and subconsciously knew there was a call on my life to pastoral ministry. After a year or so of living with the gnawing feeling that even though engineering was satisfying vocationally God had something else for me, I sought to rid myself of the feeling of frustration and confusion by going to the smartest Christian I knew with this question: *Should I become a minister or remain an engineer?* This math professor, who had memorized most of the New Testament, listened attentively to me—a twenty-three-year-old puzzled young Christian. After hearing my dilemma, he said, "David, God has lots of ministers. Serve the Lord as an engineer." I walked away relieved that I could finally put my confusion and dilemma to rest.

However, less than one week later the confusion resurfaced. I decided to take three days off from work and spend the time fasting and praying for God's wisdom. At the end of the three days of fasting and prayer, the Lord spoke to me in an audible voice and said: "David, go and preach My Word." And as they say in show business, "That's a wrap!" The issue was settled. I was to transition from engineering into ministry. My time of fasting yielded a powerful breakthrough that I'm still walking in, almost thirty-three years later.

Admittedly the breakthrough Mordecai and his fellow Jews were seeking was a greater one than mine. They needed an unretractable law to either be repealed or supernatural protection and victory should the Babylonians attack them.

**Involve decision-makers with your cry.**

Eventually news of Mordecai's distressing behavior and soul-gripping attire made its way to the queen. Queen Esther—a Jew herself—was Mordecai's young cousin. But because she was an orphan, Mordecai raised her as his own daughter. He was essentially the only father she knew. Still, although she was queen, she was totally oblivious to the new law and the impending doom of the Jews throughout the provinces of Babylon if the law was acted upon.

Moved by the news of Mordecai's state, Queen Esther sent clothes for him to put on. Without clothes he was not allowed past the king's gate, much less into the palace to speak directly with her. But Mordecai was in warrior mode. He refused to exchange his warrior's attire for nice threads. He refused to have a nice chat with Queen Esther if it was designed to get him out of battle mode. We learn from his example that if we don't guard our spiritual focus, people who are not facing our crisis and are oblivious to the impact of the crisis on their own lives will not know what it takes to draw God into the battle. Mordecai needed to stay focused on his wailing, crying, fasting, and praying to the God of heaven.

Once Mordecai explained their predicament to Queen Esther through her liaison, he encouraged her to use her position to persuade the king to intervene on their behalf. Not sharing the same sense of desperation, Queen Esther gave the lame excuse that she had not seen the king in the last thirty days. According to Persian law, if anyone—including her—approached the king in the inner court, it could mean their death. The only recourse would be if the king held out his golden scepter, signaling, "You may approach me with your concern."

Mordecai fired back this cautionary note:

> Do not think that because you are in the king's house you alone of all the Jews will escape. For if you remain silent at this time, relief and deliverance for the Jews will arise from another place, but you and your father's

family will perish. And who knows but that you have come to your royal position for such a time as this?
—ESTHER 4:13–14

Esther took the note as a call to action. Mordecai's problem was now her problem. His spiritual vigilance was now her distress. That is exactly what war cries are designed to do—move the complacent to a state of discomfort. It moves the person sitting on the sidelines into the battle.

Queen Esther formulated a strategy. Here's what she planned and communicated to Mordecai:

> Go, gather together all the Jews who are in Susa, and fast for me. Do not eat or drink for three days, night or day. I and my attendants will fast as you do. When this is done, I will go to the king, even though it is against the law. And if I perish, I perish.
>
> —ESTHER 4:16

As you can see, Esther was not unfamiliar with the weapon of prayer. You cannot enter into an absolute fast—one that calls for no food or drink—as a rookie in the world of fasting. You must have had some experience with lesser types of fasts, such as a partial fast. Esther knew her way around God's war room. Her maids did also. Mordecai certainly did. Apparently he had taught her the principle of fasting growing up in his home.

It's important to notice that Queen Esther did not rely on her natural relationship with the king—her husband—as her basis for approaching him. All too often we approach people in the strength of our earthly relationships. We must not overlook the benefit of God going before us. Esther wanted that. She needed that. Her life depended on it. The lives of all Jews in Babylon also depended on it. Esther wanted favor with the king, the kind that only God can give. She was not going to rely on her beauty, her sexual prowess, her charm, or the king's fondness and love for her. She couldn't risk a hit-or-miss scenario. She needed a surefire response. She needed the king to hold out his golden scepter to her. So she applied her faith in God by fueling her prayers with fasting.

**Involve a greater group with your cry.**

Queen Esther's strategy called for *all* the Jews in Susa to join her and *all* of her maids in the fast. Since the war cry is designed to rouse the soldiers, Mordecai's war cry was successful. It enrolled Queen Esther into the battle, and she in turn invited all of the Jews to join together in a three-day fast.

Unity in prayer adds an element of strength that would otherwise be missing. This is a unique principle to grasp. However, Jesus taught it. He said, "Again, truly I tell you that if *two* of you on earth *agree* about anything they ask for, it will be done for them by my Father in heaven. For where *two or three* gather in my name, there am I with them" (Matt. 18:19–20, emphasis added). This group approach to prayer is normally referred to as the prayer of agreement. It is built on the word *agree* as cited in the passage. *Agree* comes from the Greek word *sumphōneō* (pronounced *soom-fo-neh'-o*), which means "to be harmonious; to agree together; to agree with." It forms the English words *symphony* and *concert*. This is where we get the term *concert of prayer.*

Mordecai's war cry resulted in a three-day concert of prayer in Susa. The prayer of agreement invited God into the fray. This is why Jesus taught us how to practice this powerful type of prayer. In fact, when we use this method of prayer, Jesus says that He cannot resist its allure. He joins the prayer meeting. The prayer of agreement is irresistible to God, but the war cry often must be sounded first.

Joshua used the war cry in his day to rally the people to fighting mode. It is a surefire way to get people on point with prayer and any other form of vigilance in the face of threats. The Scripture declares: "But Joshua had commanded the army, 'Do not give a war cry, do not raise your voices, do not say a word until the day I tell you to shout. Then shout'" (Josh. 6:10)!

### Activate faith with your cry.

The memorable words of Queen Esther became etched in the souls of all the Jews in Susa. She put her faith in God on the line. Everything banked on her gaining access to the king at the end of the third day. George Müller, the English evangelist said, "The only way to learn strong faith is to endure great trials."[2] Queen Esther's bold declaration showcased her strong faith. She said, "And if I perish, I perish" (Esther 4:16).

Esther had earned the right to say these faith words. They were spoken by a kneeling warrior on the battlefield. She lived the words that Charles Spurgeon later spoke in his pulpit in England: "How dare we pray in the battle if we have never cried to the Lord while buckling on the harness!"[3] Esther was no novice when it came to prayer. She was not going to tempt the Lord by only speaking to Him during times of crisis. Prayer was her mother tongue. Mordecai had made sure of that.

Leonard Ravenhill, in his book *Why Revival Tarries* reminds us that: "No man is greater than his prayer life."[4] Esther did not struggle to remember that being on her knees gave her more power than sitting on her throne. Through her faith, Queen Esther was capturing a glimpse of what God could do. Over those three days she and the other intercessors remained focused, paying attention to their prayer goal: access to the king because of favor from the King of kings.

True faith requires focus and strict attention to the prayer goal. Keep asking yourself these questions: Why am I in God's throne room? What am I asking God for? Why did I lift up the war cry? What is at stake if the Lord doesn't answer? These are the types of questions we ask ourselves to ensure proper focus keeps us in battle mode.

## WHAT'S YOUR WAR CRY?

We've looked at the example of Mordecai and Queen Esther and have seen the large-scale impact our war cry can make on God's plans on earth. But what would that look like in *your* life? You're not a queen of a nation, I'm guessing. You're probably not a servant of a king, either. So do war cries have any place in your life? Absolutely! Before I tell you how, let me share this true story.

Stephen was in a race against the clock. Together with his wife and his seven-year-old stepdaughter, they had been living with his in-laws in a cramped apartment since he and his wife had married two years before. The lease was set to soon end. Plus it was time they found their own space. Stephen had been looking for an apartment in Orlando, Florida, but online posts and newspaper classifieds all led nowhere. Every time he found something promising, it never materialized. There was even one apartment that was available, but after the application was submitted, they were rejected due to his wife's credit history. Prior to their marriage she'd filed for bankruptcy. Although it would have been prudent to leave Stacie's name off the lease application, their dual income would prove that they could afford the unit.

In a state of utter discouragement Stephen turned to his buddy Frank for prayer. Frank was the youth pastor at his church and a strong believer. Stephen politely listened because he knew that barring a miracle, his family would have to look for emergency shelter with friends in a week's time. And he did not want that. Frank and Stephen prayed for God to work a miracle regardless of Stacie's credit history.

As providence would have it, the dispatcher on Stephen's job sent him to an apartment complex that week to clean the carpets. While unloading all of the equipment, he happened to notice a sign that read "Apartment for Rent." The place was nicer than all the other units he and Stacie had checked out and for which they'd received denial notices.

He hesitated to inquire about the unit. But because he was desperate, he had no alternative. The receptionist showed him the apartment, and he loved it. As he filled out the application she cautioned, "You and your wife need stellar credit." Over the phone Stacie encouraged him: "Let's believe God, honey."

In a few hours Stephen got word from the receptionist. The apartment was his, if he wanted it. He excitedly called Stacie and Frank announcing the answer to prayer.

Stephen's need was a type of a war cry because it was urgent. And he acted hastily by asking Frank for prayer. Stephen did not waste time reasoning, hoping, or trying to figure out what to do or how to proceed. His family's circumstance was a crisis—a battle that needed God's immediate help. Stephen's faith was activated. God showed up at the eleventh hour.

## WILL YOU HELP SOUND A SHIFT?

In the case of Mordecai, his war cry provoked Queen Esther to engage in a life-or-death battle. Her added faith led to a powerful deliverance for the Jews. At the end of the third day the golden scepter was extended to Esther. Through a series of other miracles in response to the prayers and three-day fast, Haman was hung on the very gallows he had erected to hang Mordecai. The Jews escaped annihilation because the war cry brought God into the fight.

The unretractable law was not repealed. But the king became an advocate for the Jews. He handed Mordecai his signet ring and said: "Now write another decree in the king's name in behalf of the Jews as seems best to you, and seal it with the king's signet ring—for no document written in the king's name and sealed with his ring can be revoked" (Esther 8:8). The new law written by Mordecai granted the Jews the right to bear arms and protect themselves against anyone who'd try to carry out the previous unretractable law of annihilation.

The end result is that the Jews throughout Babylon rejoiced with feasting. "People of other nationalities became Jews because fear of the Jews had seized them" (Esther 8:17). Can you believe that? The Jews got the upper hand across the nation where they were once foreigners. Only God could orchestrate this kind of outcome!

This is why we must lift up the war cry in our churches, in our communities, in our homes. This is why *you* must lift up the war cry where you are. If you would dare call others to a concert of prayer, a major shift can occur. If you would dare lead others in a concert of prayer, only God knows what shifts would occur in the world.

*Chapter 5*

# BE STRATEGIC IN
# YOUR PRAYER

A COWORKER NAMED DARIA tearfully confided in Frances that she was facing deportation. Daria's work visa had expired. The filing deadline for extension and permanent residency had long passed. Legally she no longer had the right to work in the United States. But what recourse did she have? On one hand, the thought of returning to the Ukraine, a country driven by civil and political unrest, was a frightening option. On the other hand, without a job in the United States, her family would face starvation, homelessness, and all the other horrendous problems joblessness creates. Caught between a rock and a hard place, Daria lived in constant fear each day.

With a mixture of empathy for Daria and confidence in God, Frances outlined a prayer strategy. It included the alignment of Daria's life to God's moral and behavioral standards. Daria had tearfully volunteered that she'd not been easy to live with. She'd often snap at family members and sometimes curse under her breath. All these were symptoms of the stress of not knowing her government status.

Even so, repentance is in order when our behavior and attitude are out of sync with God's Word. Sin separates us from God. Conversely repentance connects and aligns us to God. To pray expectantly, we must be mindful of this principle: "The prayer of a person living right with God is something powerful to be reckoned with" (James 5:16, THE MESSAGE). At Frances's suggestion, Daria recommitted her life to serving Jesus Christ.

The prayer strategy Frances drew up also called for a weekly day of fasting and prayer. Frances joined Daria in these set times of prayer and fasting. Their faith grew weekly as they held fast to this battle strategy.

Then everything came to a head a month later at our church's Prayerfest event. This is an annual event birthed out of Joel's prophecy that says, "Declare a holy fast; call a sacred assembly. Summon the elders and all who live in the land to the house of the LORD your God, and cry out to the LORD" (Joel 1:14). For this event, a few thousand people take a day off from work and gather to pray, worship, and receive instruction on prayer. Prayerfest has become an oasis for many as they recognize the need to cry out to the Lord in a concert of prayer.

During Prayerfest, on this particular occasion, Frances prayed for God to work a miracle for Daria. Then at 4:09 p.m., just minutes after the close of Prayerfest, Frances received an elated call from Daria. After getting an earful of joyful screaming, she was finally able to make sense of Daria's exciting news. That afternoon Daria had received a job offer from another company. Though the job required her to relocate to another state, what made this opportunity unique was that the company had agreed to use all of their business and political muscle to keep Daria in the country. They would immediately take the lead to interface with immigrations. In addition to receiving full pay during this legal process, plus an increase of 25 percent, Daria would receive free housing for eighteen months.

The fingerprint of God was all over this miracle. This was no coincidence! It was a direct answer to prayer—warfare prayer, at that.

When Frances shared this story with me, I was overjoyed on many levels. Apart from her friend's needs being met, I was encouraged by how they used prayer as a weapon. And the prayer strategy Frances formulated showed her strong grasp of the prayer tactic Jesus taught.

# THE THREEFOLD STRATEGY OF PRAYER

Together Frances and Daria grew in their understanding of prayer as a tool, a weapon, and a doorway to the ultimate power source—God. This is how you must view prayer. First, Frances connected with Daria's plight emotionally. Second, she made a sound and rational strategy to pray for a much-needed breakthrough. Third, Frances boldly and persistently brought her prayer request before God. She "knocked on the door." Jesus challenged us to take that approach when He said, "Ask and it will be given to you; seek and you will find; knock and the door will be opened to you. For everyone who asks receives; the one who seeks finds; and to the one who knocks, the door will be opened" (Luke 11:9–10).

Notice the movement of the words *ask, seek,* and *knock.* There is actually a progression of the intent of your prayer, suggesting that our prayers may be met with some sort of resistance. This resistance is evidence of the ongoing spiritual warfare we are embroiled in.

Jesus used two teaching styles to drive home this vital lesson on prayer. First, He used a story—*the parable of the friend at midnight*—which underscores the emotional and crisis-like approach that warfare praying demands. Second, Jesus offered a step-by-step explanation of the story that provides a rational, coherent lesson on the three stages of prayer.

In this spiritual war we fight against evil forces. The prayer tactic we use depends heavily on the resistance we face. Light or no resistance calls for light artillery. Heavy resistance calls for heavy artillery. Mastery of the weapon of prayer requires a working knowledge of the varying stages of warfare prayer.

## THE EMOTIONAL SIDE OF PRAYER

Jesus tells a parable that features a man surprised by a friend's visit in the middle of the night. Customarily the man would have had to prepare food for his visiting friend, regardless of the hour, because the friend had traveled quite a distance. Not providing him with a meal would be committing cultural suicide. (See Luke 11:5–8.)

But the man in the first house had no bread. In Middle Eastern society bread was used much like cutlery is used in our day. The bread was used to scoop up the meat, sop up the gravy, or pick up other side dishes. It was a staple much needed for a meal. So the man goes to a neighbor to ask for three loaves of bread.

Because of the lateness of the hour, the friend calls from behind his closed door, "I can't get up and give you anything" (v. 7). Rather than returning home empty-handed, the man continues knocking until the neighbor opens the door with bread in hand. Jesus commends the man for his boldness.

Jesus often used parables as a primary means of instructing His audience. A parable is not just a nice story that is interesting to listen to. It is a form of speech known as *rhetoric*. This type of communication is aimed at convincing its hearers to abandon their former or present perspectives and adopt the one being presented. Politicians and preachers use rhetoric all the time. Politicians use it when they are campaigning. They want to convince you to embrace their views and vote for them. Preachers like me are trying to get a listening audience to embrace a biblical view of life in lieu of other worldviews.

And the important point here is this: whoever uses rhetoric laces it with a strong emotional hook. This is where the persuasion and conversion occurs.

Under no circumstance was the first man going to return home empty-handed. Not only would he be totally embarrassed to have his friend eat in his home with bare hands, but the breadless meal would also cause the man to lose honor in the broader community, since wherever he went, the story was sure to be told and retold. You know how stories go. After each telling, it gets more embellished and exaggerated. He had to save face by knocking boldly until his request was met.

The New Testament scholar John R. Donahue adds richness to the emotional appeal of this parable by pointing out, "The man in bed does not himself want to be shamed because he turned down the request of a friend."[1] Both parties recognized that the honor of the village was at stake. Could you imagine an entire village's reputation soured because of one passerby's negative experience? In a culture of hospitality the value of friendliness and warmth must be safeguarded at all cost. That is why the man continued to shamelessly knock on his friend's door until his request was met.

Jesus is asking us to be just as brazen when it comes to prayer. We must not be so quick to abandon our request or get sidetracked at the first or even second hint of resistance. And He's showing us that when it comes to important matters of prayer, we must be driven by the emotional component that stirs us to fight and protect that which is important.

Here's an example of what I mean. When Andy's older sister, Chelsea, came to his door, she was so belligerent he had to call the police. He knew she was troubled, but this was over the top—even for Chelsea. Her loud-mouthed and aggressive behavior gripped his wife and teen daughters with fear. The peaceful environment of their home was disrupted. Up to this point Andy had shielded his family from Chelsea's drug addiction. But now he found himself having to explain to his girls why their aunt was acting so crazy. Chelsea's drug abuse was getting worse, not better.

Her problem was a problem for the entire family, well beyond her own household. Chelsea could not care for herself, much less her three kids, who were now living with extended family members.

Once the police escorted her out of his home, Andy was crippled with emotions. He was angry. He was sympathetic. And he was deeply saddened. This was his sister, after all. Before long, though, his anger toward Chelsea turned to anger toward the devil. The game-changer was when the devil said to him: "Why don't you just give up?"

Andy was shocked for a minute. But then he thought, "How dare Satan attack my sister! How dare he break up her family—my family!" Andy's rage drove him to prayer. He recognized that Chelsea needed medical and spiritual help. He was to provide the spiritual help so that she would be in a position mentally and emotionally to accept the medical help she also needed. So Andy committed to pray and fast weekly for Chelsea's freedom.

Several months later Chelsea called him and said, "Can you help me get off drugs?" She had hit rock bottom. This was the phone call Andy had been waiting for. He helped her get into a Christ-centered residential drug-treatment program out of state. She graduated the program one year later—drug free and a solid disciple of Jesus Christ. Instead of leaving the center, however, she stayed on for another six months to serve in their leadership program. In addition to finding deliverance, Chelsea had found her calling to help set others free from drug abuse through Christ.

The story doesn't end there. During the leadership program Chelsea met her future husband—a solid Christian. Not only was Andy in the wedding, he was also the minister who married them. Today Chelsea thanks him for not giving up on her. It was Andy's prayers that formed a protective hedge around her. He prayed her out of the devil's suffocating grip into the tender arms of Jesus's mercy. Chelsea's life was saved through the weapon of prayer that was wielded by her brother's love for her.

## THE RATIONAL SIDE OF PRAYER

But Jesus also highlighted the common-sense, rational side of prayer when He said, "Ask and it will be given to you; seek and you will find; knock and the door will be opened to you" (Luke 11:9). The word *ask* is followed by *seek*, which is tailed by *knock*. Each word adds a more dynamic, forceful, and vigorous approach to your prayer for God's help.

### Step 1: Ask

The word *ask* means "to desire, to call for." Imagine the host in this story walking up to his neighbor's house for bread. He doesn't want to wake the whole family, but his need is urgent, so he calls softly, as if aiming his request at his friend—the father of the house. He knew his desire for bread could not be met if he remained silent. He had to voice his need. The neighbor came calling at the unholy hour of midnight because his need was a pressing one. It could not have been anticipated, as his visitor was unexpected. Regardless, the need—any need—would go unmet if it was not met by a plea for help.

Jesus said that we are to ask. And the asking must be done in anticipation of receiving. This speaks of faith. When daredevil Nik Wallenda became the first person to walk on a tightrope across the Niagara Falls, he took steady, measured steps. On June 15, 2012, Wallenda walked eighteen hundred feet across the roaring falls. To accomplish this feat, he says he did "a lot of praying, that is for sure." And then he continued: "But you know, it's all about the concentration, the focus, and the training." Wallenda focused on succeeding and not on failing. He prayed in faith, not doubt. And his prayers were answered.[2]

In this instance Wallenda asked, and God answered. There was no resistance in the spiritual realm. There was no need for Wallenda to move his prayer efforts to the next level—the level of *seeking*, which we will explore next. When you receive an immediate answer or one that does not experience any delay, you know that the prayer effort does not call for a more intense prayer strategy.

Here's another example of the prayer that asks. Dr. Kent Brantly, a thirty-three-year-old medical missionary, moved with his young family to Liberia in October 2013 to begin a two-year term working with Samaritan's Purse. He never thought twice about the deadly Ebola virus that would later claim fifteen hundred lives throughout West Africa in just a few months; it hadn't been even a blip on the national news scene for many years. Brantly's move to Liberia came from God's call, he says, to serve the people of Liberia.[3]

Roughly six months after his arrival, Ebola was detected in Guinea and had begun to spread to Liberia. The first Ebola patient arrived several weeks later. But Brantly remained calm. He and his medical crew took care of each patient with great care and compassion. They also took every precaution to protect themselves from the dreaded disease—characterized by joint pain, diarrhea, vomiting, headache, and other debilitating, often deadly symptoms—by following the World Health Organization's guidelines for safety. To protect his family—and to devote even more time to saving lives—Brantly sent his wife and children back to the United States.

Three days later on Wednesday, July 23, 2014, Brantly woke up feeling under the weather, and in a very short time his life took an unexpected turn as he was diagnosed with the Ebola virus. As Brantly lay in bed for the following nine days, getting sicker and weaker each day, he prayed that God would help him to remain faithful even in illness. He says he also prayed that in his life or in his death, God would be glorified.

In August—after weeks of suffering from the deadly virus—Brantly did, in fact, recover. At a press conference, he said, "I did not know then, but I have learned since, that there were thousands, maybe even millions of people around the world praying for me throughout that week, and even still today. And I have heard story after story of how this situation has impacted the lives of individuals around the globe—both among my friends and family, and also among complete strangers. I cannot thank you enough for your prayers and your support. But what I can tell you is that I serve a faithful God who answers prayers."[4]

"Asking prayer" is seen as Dr. Brantly simply laid his request before God. There was no need to pursue strategy, deep insight, or any other route other than simply asking for healing.

He showered gratitude on people connected to the Samaritan's Purse, medical staff, and the Liberian community. And he added: "God saved my life—a direct answer to thousands and thousands of prayers... You cared for me and ministered to me during the most difficult experience of my life, and you did so with the love and mercy of Jesus Christ.

"Thank you... to all who lifted me up in prayer, asking for my healing and recovery. Please do not stop praying for the people of Liberia and West Africa, and for a quick end to this Ebola epidemic."[5]

You can confidently approach God and *ask* for His help. The asking phase of prayer highlights the ease of prayer. It underscores the eager willingness of God to respond to our pleas for help. That is why Jesus closed out the teaching on prayer by illustrating how eager a father is to answer his son's request for a fish. If the son asks for a fish his dad will give him a fish—not a snake or any harmful gift (Luke 11:11–13). When we ask, we should confidently wait to receive. This is what Jesus taught.

## Step 2: Seek

But not all prayers are answered suddenly. In instances when you don't receive an answer or you experience a sense of uneasiness, you may need to move your prayer efforts to the next level—*seeking*. In the parable the man's initial request for bread was met with cold silence from his friend on the other side of the door. But the man did not quit. His need was too grave.

That is the additional attitude Jesus teaches us to have when it comes to prayer. The silence of God does not necessarily translate into a *no*. It may be that we must move our prayer efforts to seeking. To *seek* means to search out, to inquire, to pursue an answer from God. This seeking after God is focused, passionate, and intense. It happens when our need is so great that we concentrate our prayer efforts on finding the mind of God—His solution, His remedy to our dilemma.

This recommended behavior is not one that promotes stubbornness or a flawed theology. It's just the opposite. The prophet Jeremiah declared, "Then you will call on me and come and pray to me, and I will listen to you. You will seek me and find me when you seek me with all your heart" (Jer. 29:12–13). God initiated the use of this approach. He invites us to seek Him. Jesus simply highlighted it as He taught on prayer.

So let's consider this idea of seeking. When my daughters were small, one of their favorite games—and mine—was hide-and-seek. When it was my turn to hide, Danielle and Jessica would count to ten. That gave me time to find a good hiding spot. They would search high and low for me. One of my favorite hiding spots was the coat closet. I would put the knee-high snow boots in front of my feet and pull the winter coats in front of me. There was no way they would find me if I did not want to be found. They would open the closet door and say, "Daddy, are you in there?" I would remain silent. (I know this may sound a bit mean, at least from little kid's perspective, but we really were having a good time.)

When they came back to the closet a second time, I would shake the coat a little. I was helping them to notice movements and unnatural things. Coats don't move by themselves. Then they would move the coats out of the way and scream, "Daddy, we see you! We found you!" I was just as excited to be found.

From a spiritual standpoint, Jesus says, "Seek and you will find." But unlike me, God is not playing childish, silly games with you. Your needs are critical and weighty. God is, however, maturing you by teaching you that He wants you to pursue Him in prayer. This method of prayer builds relationship. It deepens your confidence in the Almighty to provide you with needed help. It moves your relationship with God away from the surface and takes it into the deep waters—the place where true intimacy occurs. While seeking God, we search our hearts to determine if we've offended Him by our behavior, thoughts, or other undesirous acts. During these times of seeking, we appeal for forgiveness, cleansing, and restoration of biblical practices.

We want nothing to hinder God's willingness to answer our prayers. We want nothing to hinder the purity of our relationships with God. Seeking God gives us a focused time to accomplish what John Owen, the Puritan preacher, calls "true prayer." He says, "In true prayer, the Spirit of Christ reveals to us our own needs, so that we can take these needs to Christ."[6] If there is a need for repentance, it is brought to our attention in this extended time of seeking God. If God has a conflict with us, the Holy Spirit will make it known that we've consciously or unconsciously done something to displease God. We need to settle it before He can respond to our request.

Imagine a five-year-old boy who hurriedly runs to the dinner table and sits down. His hands are dirty from playing in the backyard and doing what little boys do outside. His mother says, "Johnnie, please wash your hands before you eat." Johnnie is annoyed and snaps, "I'll wash my hands after dinner. I'm hungry! What's the big deal? I have to take a bath tonight anyway." His father chimes in and calmly says, "Son, I don't like the way you speak to your mother. She spent a lot of time preparing this lovely dinner for us. Apologize." With reluctance and a big frown on his face, Johnnie offers a short, unsympathetic apology. He doesn't even look at his mom when he says *sorry*.

His mom's shoulders and face drop because Johnnie has repeatedly shown her disrespect over the past few weeks. In her defense, Johnnie's father says, "Son, your apology is not sincere. Go to your room and think about what you've done. There will be no supper for you since you're not able to properly apologize to your mother." Little Johnnie abruptly gets up, shoves the chair under the table, and stomps his feet in protest.

Now, while Johnnie's in his room stewing, he's still his parents' son. There's no question they love him deeply. But his mother's affection for Johnnie is not at its highest. She's been hurt.

Meanwhile, Johnnie plays with some of his video games to pass the time. Yet after a few minutes, the video distractions do not help him shake the idea that he was wrong. Johnnie opens the door of his room and bolts to the bathroom to wash his hands. Like a wounded puppy dog, he walks into the kitchen, tears streaming down his face. He walks over to his mom and gives her a warm hug. With his face turned up to hers, his eyes and facial expression echo the words that come out of his mouth: "Mom, I'm sorry. Please forgive me for being mean to you."

His mother is defenseless against little Johnnie's sincerity and tenderness. She throws her arms around him and smiles as her voice crackles with the words, "I forgive you, son." At that, his father says, "You're becoming a real man, son. Real men know how to apologize. Eat your dinner!"

When Johnnie took time to think about actions, he could see that his actions were wrong and hurtful. In the same way, our prayers fall flat when our lives are out of sync with God. Repentance clears the air. It brings us back into right relationship with the Lord. The process of seeking helps us reconnect with God on a deep, intimate level.

Furthermore, when sin or alignment is not the issue in *seeking prayer*, this kind of prayer allows us to remove the clutter and the clatter from our hearts so we can hear from heaven. We live in a noisy world. I'm speaking about the clamor caused by multiple opportunities, societal pressures, and the endless ways we're connected to the flow of information. Our smartphones, online activities, and social media activities cry out to us to keep up to date every moment of every day—a surefire way to stay disconnected from the Lord. It takes a lot of willpower and focus to purposefully unplug and hear from God.

Here's one example of what that can look like. Kris was a founding partner in an insurance business for over twenty years. Though she experienced a measure of success, the joy and excitement was no longer there. She would periodically pray and ask God for direction whenever the feeling of unhappiness or dissatisfaction reared its ugly head. But thinking that maybe it was just a phase, Kris didn't really go into a stronger mode of prayer until the thought entered her mind: "Sell the business." At that, she went deeper, spending the next two weeks praying and fasting for wisdom and clarity. Her plea was, "God, tell me what You want to do with my share of the business." After this effort was over, there was an inner resolve that was unmistakable. The business must be sold.

Kris then spent additional time asking God to prepare her partners' hearts so there would be no legal repercussions to her actions. Because of Kris's tactical prayers gained through her time of seeking God, she testified that God gave her a clean break from the business. There was no debt, no legal complications, and no relational trauma. Kris shared with me that she was freed as she learned to seek God through prayer.

It takes a lot of humility to seek God in this way. It means admitting that your level of wisdom, education, expertise, and networking skills are inadequate. In meekness you humble yourself and ask God for His help over a protracted time of pursuit. And you experience the promise Jesus made: he who seeks finds.

## Step 3: Knock

After reading the parable dozens of times, I finally came to understand why the slumbering neighbor opened his door with bread in hand. The friend's shamelessness couldn't be refused. His bold-faced behavior was undeniable. What also moved the resting neighbor was the confidence of his friend. The friend was sure his request would be honored despite the hour. He was a friend! In fact, he was a friend in need.

This is the kind of confidence Jesus urges us to have when it comes to prayer. In fact, one of Jesus's closest followers, the apostle John, confirms this, writing, "This is the confidence we have in approaching God: that if we ask anything according to his will, he hears us. And if we know that he hears us—whatever we ask—we know that we have what we asked of him" (1 John 5:14–15).

To repeatedly knock on someone's door—God's door—reflects one thing: you have confidence your knock will be answered. Jesus assures us, "Knock and the door will be opened to you" (Matt. 7:7). So the third level of prayer engagement when facing resistance is *knocking*. As we see and understand from the parable, the man's unwillingness to return home empty-handed was driven by his need, his knowledge of his friend's likely bread supply, and the nature of his relationship with the slumbering man. They were friends! Friends don't deny friends when the request can be easily met.

In the same way, we must recognize God's willingness to answer our prayers. Knocking on His door suggests that we oppose spiritual forces through a concentrated time of soul-searching, fasting, and focused prayers. These disciplines are all part and parcel of warfare praying. They are not the arm-twisting behavior of Christians attempting to manipulate God. That's normative Christianity. Jesus invites us to knock until the door is opened. In His humanity He often fasted and went on private prayer retreats to discern the will of God. These times of prevailing prayer also provided Him with the needed strength to do the will of God. Are you willing to engage God on that level?

In his book *Crazy Love* Francis Chan writes, "I quickly found that the American church is a difficult place to fit in if you want to live out New Testament Christianity. The goals of American Christianity are often a nice marriage, children who don't swear, and good church attendance. Taking the words of Christ literally and seriously is rarely considered. That's for the 'radicals' who are 'unbalanced' and who go 'overboard.' Most of us want a balanced life that we can control, that is safe, and that does not involve suffering."[3] I couldn't have said it better. We are in a high-stakes spiritual war. We must see ourselves as soldiers in combat. Luxury and civilian-like living is not our posture. It's vital that we take seriously the teachings of Jesus as it relates to prayer. God is willing to do His part. He's willing to open His coffers and grant our requests. We must do our part. Knock in prayer!

And now I'll share with you a story of what knocking prayer looks like. At some of our worship events, we often have someone share their story of how they journeyed to faith in Christ. Within three to four minutes the church family is taken through the maze of someone's life. The story ends at the cross where we learn how they exchanged their sins for Jesus's righteousness.

At one particular Good Friday event, a woman named Sandy was slated to tell her story between some of the song selections. She is a member of our staff and a deaconess in our church, and she is well loved by all because of her Christlike attitude. There are just some Christians you encounter who make it incredibly hard to picture their ever living a reckless life—a life apart from God. Sandy is one of those people. To hear her story was an eye-opener for me.

Sandy grew up in the 1950s. According to her there was an epidemic of polio in her neighborhood. Adults and children alike were dying left and right. She was the youngest of eight siblings. Before her fourth birthday she was stricken with polio. Shortly after the diagnosis she fell deathly ill and quickly became bedridden. Her legs became paralyzed.

In those days polio was incurable. Once stricken the victim would experience spasms, high fever, and then paralysis of the limbs. Without a miracle, Sandy's next stop was death's door. The dreaded notice was nailed on the front door of her house: "Contagious disease in this house. Quarantine." This notice was like a death sentence. No one was allowed in her bedroom except her mother and the visiting nurse. Because of the finality of the infectious disease, Sandy knew loneliness and darkness. She couldn't see or talk with her siblings. They weren't allowed in her room. The window curtains were kept closed.

As Sandy explained how polio kept her in a delirious state due to the high fever, we sat on the edge of our seats, eager to learn what brought about her miracle. How could this beautiful, poised woman with an adult son have ever have been so sick?

Sandy engaged our hearts as she matter-of-factly told her story. She shared that when a few of the praying women from the neighborhood church learned about her plight, they made arrangements to visit her. They were not looking to show sympathy, to empathize with her parents, or to bring some delicious-tasting snacks that would momentarily ease her pain. They wanted to pray. Their sole mission was to knock on God's door on Sandy's behalf.

Sandy said, "The ladies told my mother that they would not leave the house until God healed me. 'Last week a child died from polio a block away,' they shared. 'We're not going to stand by and see another child die!' True to their word, they never left until I walked out of the bed healed."

Since they were not allowed into Sandy's bedroom, they prayed from the downstairs kitchen.

"Their prayers were different than I was accustomed to," Sandy testified. She says they prayed with indignation—a righteous anger. They prayed confidently. They prayed shamelessly. They prayed without a hint of the possibility of denial. They prayed as if they knew God intimately. They prayed with knowledge of their authority in Christ. And they wielded their authority with grace. It was as if they were calling upon their familiar Friend at the midnight hour.

Sandy shared, "At a certain point in their prayers, the miracle occurred. I didn't feel anything unusual or have an unfamiliar sensation flush through my body. Although I could not quite comprehend it, I knew God healed me. Immediately I went from having the worst form of polio to walking. I knew it had everything to do with the relentless prayers of these women. They kept knocking and knocking and knocking on God's door until He opened it."

The ladies handed Sandy a healing just like the neighbor was handed the loaves of bread in the parable. She said, "At four years old I became aware of God's love for me. A few years later I learned of salvation through Christ. I accepted Jesus as my Savior when I was eleven."

Our faith as a church was buoyed that Good Friday. We were reminded once again of the power and value of the weapon of prayer. What kept swirling around in my mind was Paul's declaration:

> For though we live in the world, we do not wage war as the world does. The weapons we fight with are not the weapons of the world. On the contrary, they have divine power to demolish strongholds. We demolish arguments and every pretension that sets itself up against the knowledge of God, and we take captive every thought to make it obedient to Christ.
>
> —2 CORINTHIANS 10:3–5

Have you tried knocking when you pray? I mean, is there a nagging situation in your life right now that you have not faced with this level of spiritual fire power? Don't allow resistance to stop you from warfare praying. The weapon of prayer is unlike any weapon of this world. It has divine power—power that will annihilate anything Satan throws at you, no matter how powerful it appears. Jesus gave us a proven plan. He said, "To the one who knocks, the door will be opened" (Luke 11:10).

Notice the attitude and the behavior of the praying ladies in Sandy's story. Before they prayed, they had a shamelessness and indignation. Denial was not an option. In confidence they approached Sandy's mother with the promise, "We're not leaving your house until the child is healed." With equal confidence they approached God.

When the level of prayer moves up the scale to knocking, it calls for an assurance that is steeped in an almost unimaginable confidence in God. To pray this way, you have to know that your relationship with God is in right standing. You pray from a place of "pleasing God." It's where friends of God stand to pray. It's where people who walk in communion with God stand to pray. I'm not talking about perfect people, because there are none. I'm speaking of forgiven people. They enjoy uninterrupted fellowship with God. If you don't have that now, you can. It begins and ends with living a life where your confession of sin is kept current.

When our scheduled payments for our cars, our homes, and other big-ticket items are kept current, we enjoy using those things in our lives. Similarly if we keep our confession current with God, we are assured to walk in the light—the place where uninterrupted communion occurs.

People who know how to knock in prayer are a special breed of soldiers—the kind who never go without repenting of sin. If they sin, they quickly confess it, repent of it, and forsake it. They don't want to be out of alignment with God for any reason. This kind of vigilance for your spiritual health says to God, "I want to constantly please You." God in turn says, "When a man's ways are pleasing to the LORD, he makes even his enemies to be at peace with him" (Prov. 16:7, NAS). When you please God, you can confidently approach Him in prayer. You will not be denied.

Lastly, it's helpful to know that this kind of prayer that knocks at God's door often includes some element of fasting. The reason why fasting is such a great companion to prayer is because it is an appeal to God for help. Jesus taught:

> When you fast, do not look somber as the hypocrites do, for they disfigure their faces to show others they are fasting. Truly I tell you, they have received their *reward* in full. But when you fast, put oil on your head and wash your face, so that it will not be obvious to others that you are fasting, but only to your Father, who is unseen; and your Father, who sees what is done in secret, will *reward* you.
> —MATTHEW 6:16–18, EMPHASIS ADDED

Jesus allows us to peek behind the heavenly veil and learn that fasting catches God's eye. God sees when we deliberately choose to abstain from eating for spiritual purposes. He then interprets our fasting as a direct request—a type of prayer of the soul—for His help. Jesus concluded that God will reward us after we've fasted. The word *reward* here means "to perform, render, restore, and to give or do something necessary in fulfillment of an obligation or expectation." Since God promised to reward us when we fast, these praying ladies added fasting to their prayers. And true to His Word, God showed up and healed Sandy. That was their reward.

## APPLY STRATEGY
## TO YOUR PRAYERS

I encourage you to not allow Satan to strong-arm you. Take Jesus's words to heart: "Ask and it will be given to you; seek and you will find; knock and the door will be opened to you. For everyone who asks receives; the one who seeks finds; and to the one who knocks, the door will be opened" (Luke 11:9–10).

Human beings are God's highest creation. We can feel, think, reason, and even strategize. But in the arena of spiritual warfare we seldom apply reason and strategy to our prayers. Strategizing is needed and should not be left solely for use in business or other natural arenas. I'm not suggesting that we can outwit or outmaneuver Satan by our prayers. We cannot. We're not called or tasked to do that! And we don't need to since God is the one who fights on our behalf.

We are called to grow, develop, and mature in every area of life, which includes prayer. In the natural mature people get to their destination faster than their immature counterparts.

The mature ones know how to draw wisdom from their experiences, promised futures, and strategic partnerships.

Information can help you be more strategic with your prayers. For example, having a medical report that details your sickness allows you to pray strategically for your healing. Some choose to simply pray in a generalized way without any information whatsoever. Although God is not limited by our lack of information about our case, praying from a place of knowledge boosts our faith. Information allows us to know how to pray through each step of the process until the miracle is fully realized.

If we apply the principle of strategizing to our prayers, we should be able to maximize our results while minimizing our frustrations. Being clear minded and self-controlled helps us not only to pray, but also to pray more strategically (1 Pet. 4:7). To become clear minded you have to set aside uninterrupted time to seek God. You cannot pray strategically if you're running from one emergency to another. Or if your schedule is so tight that your mind is cluttered with an extensive to-do list, strategic praying goes out the window.

As you bring greater balance to your life and schedule, you will automatically reap the benefits in your prayer life. Your prayers will become more effective and more strategic.

*Chapter 6*

# PRAYER AS DEFENSE

S EVERAL YEARS AGO, the sports clothing company Under Armour blazed the slogan, "Protect this house!" Usually the slogan would accompany a bulked-up athlete—an iconic symbol of someone easily able to "protect his house" from any visiting team. Similarly, at every level of sporting event, from middle school intramurals to the pro teams, cheerleaders and fans alike chant a similar refrain: "Protect this house!" It's a call to action. It's a call to dig deep. It's a call to turn up the heat. It's a call for the home team to bring their A game. It's a call for them to win. You'll also hear fans shout: "Defense!" The chant suggests their team is being outplayed or outscored. The opponent needs to be stopped, shut down, put in their place. The home team must rally to defend reputation and house.

The weapon of prayer holds just as powerful a distinction. It can be used defensively. It can also be used offensively. Paul illustrated both uses of the weapon of prayer when he said, "Devote yourselves to prayer, being watchful and thankful. And pray for us, too, that God may open a door for our message, so that we may proclaim the mystery of Christ, for which I am in chains" (Col. 4:2–3). Being watchful is a defensive stance. And the call to strategically pray that an open door occurs is an offensive approach to prayer.

This chapter will look deeply at how we ought to use the defensive approach. The following chapter will focus on the offensive use of the weapon of prayer.

## GOD IS LOOKING FOR DEFENDERS

Defensive prayers are aimed at blocking, thwarting, and undoing Satan's plans and attacks. The mere fact we're told to "take up the shield of faith, with which you can extinguish all the flaming arrows of the evil one" (Eph. 6:16) makes it clear that Christians can come under demonic attack. Satan can—and does—go on the offense by shooting arrows at us. Arrows represent temptation and any other instrument designed to trip us up. His attack is an automatic ploy to place us on the defense. When we're placed in that position, our prayers must take on a defensive tone. We must *protect this house!*

Being put on the defensive is not necessarily an indicator of our weakness or laxity. Jesus was forced into a defensive mode when He fasted in the desert for forty days. Satan attacked Him three times in an attempt to sabotage His future. But Jesus countered the deceiver's temptations with words of faith. (See Luke 4:1–13.) These words stopped Satan dead in his tracks. The barrage of attacks ended this way: "When the devil had finished all this tempting, he left him *until an opportune time*" (Luke 4:13, emphasis added). Jesus was successful with His defensive actions in this instance. But the Scripture gives a hint that Satan would be back to try again. We're told he left Jesus "until an opportune time."

If Satan can place Jesus in defense mode, why not you? No one is exempt! The fact is, strong and weak believers alike can be placed on the defensive. When a strong Christian is placed on the defensive, she quickly goes into a fighting mode. This person schedules special times of intercession and waiting on God. She does not allow Satan to run havoc in her life by succumbing to depression, pity, or worry. This is not her first time at the rodeo. Conversely, if the victim of Satan's assault doesn't know how to fight in the spiritual realm or care enough to defend their turf, she will be attacked, dominated, and aggressively subdued. That kind of complacency becomes a lifestyle of anemic Christianity, and anemic Christianity is not biblical Christianity. It is a watered-down life filled with knowledge of a few Bible verses, infrequent church attendance, and an overall defeated attitude. No one wants that! Therefore, we must become skilled at defensive praying.

Like the US Armed Forces, God is always on the lookout for a few good men—and women. He's scouting for those who'll make good kneeling warriors, defenders of their cities and their people. Ezekiel broadcasted God's search when he prophesied, "I looked for someone among them who would *build up the wall* and stand before me in the gap on behalf of the land so I would not have to destroy it, but I found no one" (Ezek. 22:30, emphasis added).

Imagine that—God did not have the prophet prophesy that He's looking to recruit preachers! That's not to say preachers are unnecessary. They're quite important. But God's search was for defenders, people who would stand guard on the wall to defend the city against any unsuspecting attack. This is why Charles Spurgeon said, "I would rather teach one man to pray than ten men to preach."[1]

By reading this book, you may be answering the cry of God's heart. He's been pursuing you as a recruiter. You'd make a good catch as a defender of your city and your family. Stop running. Accept His offer.

## MEET EPAPHRAS, THE DEFENDER

Epaphras, who is one of you and a servant of Christ Jesus, sends greetings. He is always wrestling in prayer for you, that you may stand firm in all the will of God, mature

and fully assured. I vouch for him that he is working
hard for you and for those at Laodicea and Hierapolis.
—COLOSSIANS 4:12–13

Tucked away in the New Testament are a few verses that
highlight how a man named Epaphras defensively used the
weapon of prayer. He is a legendary defender of his city and
the people living in his region. Once we piece together the
information we have about Epaphras, a wonderful biograph-
ical sketch emerges. That biography, along with his prayer
habits, show us how he served as a defender by offering protective prayers.

First, we notice that the name *Epaphras* appears only three
times in the Bible: twice in the Book of Colossians (1:7; 4:12)
and once in Philemon (1:23), another one of Paul's letters.
Epaphras is the shortened form for Epaphroditus. The latter
name represents a person cited in the Book of Philippians
but it is not the same man we're examining. They are two
different people.

Epaphras was a hard worker for Christ and the people of
God. In Paul's letter to Philemon Paul said, "Epaphras, my
*fellow prisoner* in Christ Jesus sends you greetings" (Philem.
1:23, emphasis added). New Testament scholars speculate
about Paul's meaning behind the use of the term *fellow prisoner.* There is much debate about whether or not Epaphras
shared Paul's imprisonment at some time. What is certain is
that Epaphras was more than a fellow Christian to the great
apostle.

Although Epaphras did not share the same level of gifting,
influence, or notoriety as Paul, he was a strong disciple of
Jesus Christ and of great value to Paul. For this reason, Paul
describes Epaphras as "our dear fellow servant, who is a

faithful minister of Christ on our behalf" (Col. 1:7). The word *servant* here is *doulos* (Greek), meaning "bondslave." This type of slave performs exceptionally in contrast to the other types of slaves, based strictly on Paul's choice of Greek words for *slave*.

When someone of Paul's stature publicly compliments another's faithfulness, that says something significant about that person. Paul's characterization of Epaphras is that he was dependable, trustworthy, consistent, and loyal. You could count on him! In our day such praise would be akin to writing a letter of recommendation or putting your own name behind someone.

What we learn from the fourth chapter of Colossians is most revealing of the ministry and character of Epaphras. We learn he was a native of the city of Colosse. This gave that city a special place in his heart from which to serve and pray. We learn that even while he was away from that city, he was guarding it in fervent prayer.

The most significant thing we learn about Epaphras is that he was a man of prayer. The way in which he prayed—the intensity and regularity of it—caused Paul to say, "I vouch for him that he is working hard for you and for those at Laodicea and Hierapolis" (Col. 4:13). Epaphras was a kneeling warrior who protected the Christians under his watch through the defensive use of the weapon of prayer.

Before you can become skilled at praying defensively, you must care deeply about the people or the territory you plan to protect in prayer. Whoever heard of someone using a weapon to protect people they despise or feel neutral about? I haven't! People fight for people they love and value. Even if the person is a total stranger, you protect them because you have a humanitarian love for them. Epaphras prayed for the people of Colosse from a heart of care and love.

# HOW DID EPAPHRAS PRAY?

If the apostle Paul references the prayer ministry of Epaphras, this guy must have been exceptional. Paul himself was a man of prayer. He knew people of the same ilk. Like the disciple of Jesus asked: "Lord, teach us how to pray" (Luke 11:1), had we lived in that era we would have said to Epaphras: "Teach us how to pray." By looking at Paul's description of Epahpras's prayer, we learn how he prayed and what he prayed for. Specifically we learn that when he labored in prayer, he wrestled in prayer, focused on his assignment, and remained watchful.

**He wrestled in prayer.**

To offer a word picture to the recipients of his letter, Paul borrowed from the games of track and field. Those athletes were contending for prizes—trophies in recognition of their remarkable feats of athleticism. Likewise, Paul says Epaphras was striving, competing, and battling in prayer. The act of wrestling—the hand-to-hand type—depicts the heavy-duty work needed to defeat your opponent. Wrestlers would tussle back and forth until one was weakened and eventually subdued. The role of an intercessor is to get the victory in prayer so that it materializes in the natural.

Consider this example of wrestling in prayer. Jack and Antoinette, active ministry leaders, had to turn up the heat in their prayer lives when their baby became violently ill. Julia was just a few months old and over fourteen hours had vomited almost hourly. Jack was at work when he received the call from his wife. After speaking with the pediatrician, she was told to take Julia to the emergency room. Jack rushed out of the office to drive his wife and baby to the hospital. He was not panicking though the situation was threatening. As he drove home, he wrestled in prayer for Julia's healing. Her fever had climbed to 105 according to Antoinette.

Jack had been feeding his soul with teaching and Bible memorization about divine healing for the past day and a half. He saw the need to get stronger for the sake of his family. The moment he arrived home, he laid hands on little Julia and prayed for her healing. Once they reached the hospital, the doctor took her temperature and went through a battery of tests. Not only was Julia's temperature down to 99 degrees, but she had also begun to make the appropriate baby sounds signaling her desire to be nursed. Her appetite returned, and all were shocked and overjoyed. God had healed Julia. The turnaround came when Jack stepped into his role as defender of his family and wrestled in prayer for her healing. Today Julia is eleven years old and enjoys a full life.

**He focused on his assignment.**

When Hudson Taylor was a young man in England, he came to the realization one day: "When I get to China…I shall have no claim on anyone for anything. My only claim will be on God. How important to learn, before leaving England, to move man, through God, by prayer alone….My kind employer wished me to remind him whenever my salary became due. This I determined not to do directly, but to ask that God would bring the fact to his recollection, and thus encourage me by answering prayer."[2]

Hudson's goal and vocational objective was to be a missionary to China. He eventually went to China and later founded the China Inland Mission, a group instrumental in bringing more than eight hundred missionaries into China. He was focused on his assignment. Because of that he needed to cultivate a certain level of spiritual strength before embarking on such a journey. Otherwise he would languish overseas being unprepared spiritually due to an undeveloped prayer life. The principle that Epaphras mastered, namely, staying focused on his assignment through prayer, is what Hudson Taylor practiced. He shared, "The question uppermost in my mind was, 'Can I go to China, or will my want of faith and power with God prove so serious an obstacle as to preclude my entering upon this much-prized service?'"[3] That is how you utilize prayer to help you stay focused on your divine assignment.

Epaphras was an extremely focused leader! The letter Paul wrote to the Colossians was written in response to a situation Epaphras had relayed to Paul. The damaging teaching and propaganda of a gnostic sect was becoming a growing problem for the believers in Colosse and the neighboring twin cities, Laodicea and Hierapolis. Gnostics create confusion in the minds of immature believers by mixing philosophical ideas into the Christian faith. The end result is an impure faith pieced together by the views of different ideological camps. So the wisdom and advice Paul offered to the Colossians in the letter had been solicited by Epaphras.

While spending time with Paul, Epaphras did not overlook his responsibility to be a defender of his congregation through prayer. According to New Testament scholars, including Richard C. H. Lenski, Epaphras was the founder of the Colossian congregation and possibly the other two churches of Laodicea and Hierapolis.[4] They were in his heart so much so that even when apart from them physically and geographically, they were his focus in prayer. They were his assignment from God. He guarded them this way.

**He remained watchful.**

Epaphras was always in prayer for his congregation. His watchfulness over them in prayer was not sporadic or incidental. Paul vouched for him that he was *always* wrestling in prayer for them. He was consumed with his role as a defender. His prayers focused on their welfare. This wasn't an episodic activity. It was an ongoing one.

I can connect to this when I think about what happened when our children were away at college. Marlinda and I chose Wednesdays as a day of prayer and fasting for them. We would meet for an hour in the afternoon to pray together for their protection, their ongoing spiritual growth, their clarity of mind, and the like. We certainly prayed independently of each other over the course of the week, but we isolated Wednesdays to "defend our house" through this concert of prayer. Praise God! It has been a number of years since they graduated and moved into their career paths. But looking back, we rejoice because it was through our prayers that they were safeguarded and protected. They graduated with their faith intact, with good grades, and emotionally prepared to face the next phase of their lives.

## WHAT DID EPAPHRAS PRAY FOR?

So we've learned *how* Epaphras prayed, but *what* did he pray for when he prayed? Paul indicated Epaphras focused his prayers on three critical areas, each having to do with what makes for a strong Christian—that they would "stand firm in the will of God, mature and fully assured" (Col. 4:12). Each of these areas requires full protection in order to safeguard the spiritual health and success of the recipient.

**That they would stand firm in God's will**

If you are going to experience any measure of success in your relationship with God, you must live in the security of God's will. Believers must be especially focused on pleasing God by living in the center of His will. Knowing God's will and accepting to live in harmony with it is the best possible, most satisfying life you could ever have. My friend Dr. R. T. Kendall often says, "The happiest pillow on which you may rest your head is the knowledge of God's will. I cannot imagine a more miserable situation than consciously to be out of God's will." I say amen to that.

Though living in the will of God is rudimentary to the Christian faith, Epaphras had his finger on the pulse of his community. They needed spiritual protection—the kind that must be undergirded and safeguarded through prayer. So he prayed for those in Colosse, Laodicea, and Hierapolis to stand firm in all the will of God. The fact that he prayed for them not just to *know* the will of God, but also to *stand firm* in it reveals an important point. This kneeling warrior was interested in the believers' ability to accept the will of God with great assurance and joy. Some people accept the will of God as if God was pointing a loaded gun in their direction accompanied by the words, "Accept My will or else!" This attitude leads to resentment and a constant battle with disobedience. Epaphras wanted to protect his fellow believers from this nerve-wracking struggle. So he took to a place of prayer—a defensive place.

In his book *The Hole in Our Gospel* Richard Stearns talks about how he transitioned from CEO of Lenox China to become the president of World Vision.[5] These companies couldn't be further apart from each other in purpose, mission, and operating platform. Lenox is a profit-based corporation that sells high-end china and tableware mostly to wealthy consumers. World Vision is a nonprofit corporation focused on global relief efforts to the poor. Naturally Stearns was baffled when a recruiter reached out to him to talk about heading World Vision.

Stearns admitted that he openly laughed at the idea and quickly rattled off the stark differences between the two companies. But the recruiter was undaunted, saying, "Would you just keep an open mind?" Stearns's reply was, "Not really." Then the recruiter changed his approach and simply said, "Let me ask you a different question: Are you willing to be open to God's will for your life?"

Those words meant the world to Stearns. He agreed to pray about it.

At first the thought of praying about this opportunity seemed preposterous to Stearns. On the surface, Stearns said, "Surely, God couldn't be in it." Yet because he promised to pray about the possibility in light of being willing to be open to God's will, he prayed. And something surprising happened. The Lord's will was revealed. The rest is history. In 1998 Rich Stearns became the president of World Vision US, one of the world's largest nonprofit humanitarian organizations. When your will is God's will, Spurgeon says, you will have your will.

### That they would stand in maturity

One of my spiritual heroes is Billy Graham. I love how self-lessly he's lived his entire life. I had the privilege of serving on the executive committee for the final Billy Graham Crusade—the one held in New York City in 2005. During a special and closed time of sharing with some two hundred fifty workers at that event, myself included, Dr. Graham gave us a few words of advice drawn from his lengthy tenure in ministry. One of the things he said, which he often writes in his books, was that he wished he had more education.

This longing brought me back to something I read in his autobiography, *Just As I Am*. During his early days of international ministry and overseas travel, he had a speaking engagement at the prestigious University of Cambridge in Great Britain. He was encouraged by his friend Hugh Gough, "Do not regard these men as 'intellectuals.' Appeal to their conscience. They are sinners, needing a Savior. Conviction of sin, not intellectual persuasion, is the need."[6]

In spite of this caution Graham says he worked diligently to "put the gospel into an intellectual framework in eight messages."[7] Graham writes: "For the first three nights of the public meetings, beginning on Sunday…I felt as if I were in a straight-jacket on the platform, and very little happened…Then, on my knees with a deep sense of failure, inadequacy, and helplessness, I turned to God. My gift, such as it was, was not to present the intellectual side of the Gospel. I knew that. What those students needed was a clear understanding of the simple but profound truths of the Gospel: our separation from God because of sin; Christ's provision of forgiveness and new life; and our hope because of Him."[8]

Graham continued, "Finally, on the Wednesday night, I threw away my prepared address and preached a simple Gospel message on the meaning of the Cross of Christ. That night more than 400 Cambridge students stayed behind to make their commitment to Christ."[9]

After reading this account, I rejoiced that Dr. Graham was able to adjust his gospel appeal midstream. Without that, he would not have seen the result that happened that Wednesday night. More telling, however, is the fact that back then he was not standing in the level of maturity in which he was standing that afternoon in front of the two hundred fifty leaders in New York City. When he mentioned his wish for more education, it was not with regret, disappointment, or bitterness. Neither was there a hint of internal striving borne out of self-rejection. Fifty years ago, Dr. Graham wanted to prove something to those "Cambridge men." That was no longer the case.

This is the very thing that Epaphras was fighting against in prayer. He wanted to protect his people from the traps of immaturity. One such trap is the unwillingness to accept yourself, your gifts, your personality, and the way God wired you. Therefore Epaphras prayed in a protective manner that they would stand in maturity.

How many people do you know who have collapsed under pressure—family pressure, financial pressure, or pressure on the job? Too many! Had we prayed for God to "protect their house" so that they would stand in maturity, perhaps the collapse would have been averted.

I am not trying to place blame or guilt on your shoulders. I'm simply pointing out that there is a responsibility to pray defensively for those within our sphere. It's our job. It's the greatest way we can show our love to our friends, coworkers, and family. For this very reason, Charles H. Spurgeon said, "The man who is mighty in prayer may be a wall of fire around his country, her guardian angel and her shield."[10]

## That they would stand fully assured

A fully assured person is a confident person. They no longer question or second guess the rightness of their actions or decisions. The term *fully assured* means "to be complete" or "to be fully convinced." Epaphras's thinking was: When a believer is absolutely certain of God's will, nothing can hold them back. If adversity comes their way, the fact that they know they're in the will of God, will be of great service. If you're fighting for the will of God, all heaven stands behind you. But if you are unsure as to where God stands on the matter, your enthusiasm and ability to fight drops significantly.

The logic behind Epaphras's prayer was a stroke of genius. This kneeling warrior was placing a protective shield around his congregation and the other churches to which he had some pastoral responsibility. He knew the power of conviction. The place of certainty is a high ground from which battles can be won. Faith springs from certainty. You cannot have faith without a deep sense of certainty and assurance. Conversely the place of uncertainty and doubt is the place where battles are lost, dreams are aborted, and hope is short lived.

People who vacillate between certainty and uncertainty (or faith and doubt) is what James described as being "like a wave of the sea, blown and tossed by the wind" (James 1:6). The metaphor is not the most frightened part of James's discourse. The result is. We are told that the person being tossed about by uncertainty can be certain of only one thing. Their prayers will not be answered by God! (See James 1:7–8.) Epaphras was being rather strategic in his prayers, knowing the value of living in full assurance of the will of God.

Many years ago my counsel was sought by this married man whom I'll call Alex. Alex had been married for the past nineteen years, and he and his wife had four children. Alex became troubled by the question: "Is Vicky the one for me?" Can you believe this? He's now asking that question a few months before their twentieth wedding anniversary. There had not been any infidelity on either of their parts. There was no brewing crisis other than the normal stressors in marriage—meeting the needs of the kids, maintaining romantic love—you know. Alex's question would not go away. It kept on gnawing at him. He could not stand fully assured that he was in the will of God. They eventually divorced because he could not rest in any certainty or assurance that his marriage was the will of God for him.

It was painful for me to hear Alex speak of his uncertainty toward his marriage, and it was more painful for me to learn of his divorce. This experienced convinced me more than ever that I must follow Epaphras's example and pray for the people in my sphere so that they may stand fully assured in all the will of God.

Chapter 7

# PRAYER AS OFFENSE

TEARS STREAMED DOWN Marco's face as he and his wife, Michele, watched *Extreme Makeover: Home Edition*. The popular television program gifts a deserving family with a newly renovated house on each episode as the show's producers gather friends and neighbors of the selected family to lend some sweat equity to a team of paid contractors. This particular episode featured a couple who had three biological sons and several adopted children. Their home was way too cramped to comfortably accommodate the new children, much less the rest of the family. The father was also battling cancer. When the newly expanded house was complete with additional bedrooms, living space, new furnishings, appliances, and more, the family moved in. Tragically the father died having never seen the completion of the house.

After watching the episode, Marco turned to Michele and said, "I don't have a lot of money to do something like that for a needy family. But I do have lots of love. I wouldn't mind adopting a child. What do you think, sweetheart?"

Before answering, Michele ran to get her journal. She rejoined Marco in the living room with her finger on the page where she'd made a prayer entry over a year ago. It read, "God, please deal with Marco's heart so that he would join me in the desire to adopt a child. I want him to initiate the idea of adopting even though we already have three boys of our own. This way he's not doing something because of his love for me or out of obligation or pressure. Put the idea in his heart, God."

Michele's written statement didn't need any spoken words to accompany it. Her strategic prayers were answered by God. She and Marco fell into each other's arms and simply wept.

One year later a beautiful three-month old baby girl, Abigail, came into their lives. Today their family can't remember life without Abbie—the name they affectionately call her.

## WHAT IS OFFENSIVE PRAYER?

Michele's prayer in her journal was a form of offensive prayer—a prayer that seeks to take new territory for the kingdom of God. These prayers are opposite in intention and aim from defensive prayers, which seek to guard and protect your present resources and territory. Offensive prayers seek to advance your life, your ministry, and the penetration of the gospel message into the world around you. They are not reactionary. They are not backward-looking. They are not prayed in a counteractive way. Offensive prayers initiate action. They call for forward movement. They are driven by tactical steps that preclude any problem, cut off or reduce future distractions, and annihilate satanic schemes designed to trip you up.

Jesus demonstrated this type of prayer throughout His ministry. On one such occasion we read, "One of those days Jesus went out to a mountainside to pray, and spent the night praying to God. When morning came, he called his disciples to him and chose twelve of them, whom he also designated apostles" (Luke 6:12–13). In this instance Jesus was not reacting to a crisis or any kind of deterrent to His ministry. Rather, He needed God's insight as to which of His disciples should be selected as apostles. There were to be twelve. *Apostle* is a word that captures the idea of a person who's been sent on a mission with definite authority.

Jesus spent the night praying for wisdom, clarity, and knowledge of God's selection. The mission of the church was at stake. These men were going to be the foundation of the

Lord's Church. Jesus had one chance to get it right. And He did. Even Judas was God's choice. (I don't believe God predestined Judas to be a betrayer. Judas had a choice. God did, however, have foreknowledge that Judas would succumb to temptation and wind up betraying Christ for thirty pieces of silver.) The point is that Jesus saw the need to go on the offense with His prayers. And if we're going to maximize our effectiveness in the kingdom of God, we must do the same.

Charles Finney, a renowned evangelist, led hundreds of thousands of people to the kingdom of God through his ministry. But often historians overlook the way he used prayer as an offensive weapon. He often took long prayer walks in the woods. During those times he would seek God's will to organize revivals so they'd launch successfully and continue for long stretches. Finney saw prayer as a key to unlocking the outpouring of the Holy Spirit and the route to transforming society. Finney would send one of his intercessors, Father Nash, as an advance man to the cities of upcoming campaigns. Father Nash's task? Pray for days, or in some instances weeks ahead, for the hardened hearts of the community to become receptive to the gospel message. Once Finney showed up to conduct his meetings, people would have a God-consciousness that Finney attributed to Nash's times in prayer. Might I add that Father Nash was praying tactically, strategically, and offensively for the coming move of God. He was praying in anticipation of what could happen if God showed up in that city. How we need to know the power of praying offensively in these days too!

In the book *Revival Praying* Leonard Ravenhill writes of meeting an old lady who told him a story about Charles Finney and his ministry in Bolton, England. Before any preaching began in her city, he writes of her story, "Two men knocked on the door of her humble cottage, wanting lodgings. The poor woman looked amazed, for she had no extra accommodation. Finally, for about twenty-five cents a week, the two men—none other than Fathers Nash and [Abel] Clery—rented a dark and damp cellar for the period of the Finney meetings (at least two weeks), and there in that self-chosen prison cell, those prayer partners battled the forces of darkness."[1]

The same type of prayer is needed in our day. As soldiers in God's army, our approach must include offensive attacks against the kingdom of darkness and not just defensive measures to protect ourselves from its encroachment on our turf.

## WHY ARE OFFENSIVE PRAYERS NEEDED?

Weapons serve various purposes. What army can claim victory if their weaponry is made exclusively for defensive combat? Now if you want only to protect your land, your people, and your valuables from intruders, then you can claim victory when that occurs. But that has never been the goal of the army of God! We have been given the Great Commission, which is a soul-winning, turf-taking, kingdom-expansion directive. It is an offensive commission. Jesus's final words to His disciples were:

> Therefore go and make disciples of all nations, baptizing them in the name of the Father and of the Son and of the Holy Spirit, and teaching them to obey everything I have commanded you. And surely I am with you always, to the very end of the age.
> —MATTHEW 28:19–20

We have never been charged to maintain the status quo or simply protect our current possessions. That is not our charge. That is not our DNA. Jesus wants to bring lost sheep—all of them—into His fold. God wants a large family. These objectives require offensive maneuvering.

In that same vein Luke the physician writes that Jesus said, "But you will receive power when the Holy Spirit comes on you; and you will be my witnesses in Jerusalem, and in all Judea and Samaria, and to the ends of the earth" (Acts 1:8). Even the foundational Scripture about the gift of the Holy Spirit reaffirms that our calling is to share our faith *everywhere* people exist. Evangelism in and of itself is an offensive exercise. It's not good enough for us to simply grow in Christlikeness within the safety of the four walls of the church. We must reach out and draw others to Christ.

The army of God calls for offensive living. We cannot thrive at offensive living without becoming skilled at offensive praying. If we are going to venture beyond the walls of our faith, offensive praying is critical.

The idea of praying offensively had never occurred to Frank, an assistant basketball coach. But all that changed when he was forced to deal with a problem that could harm the future of a lot of people. The head coach had a drinking problem. He would often come to practice drunk. He abused the team with profanity-laced verbal attacks, insanely long practices, and other alcohol-fueled bouts that were affecting the kids' psyches and the team culture. Despite his behavior, the team reigned as regional contenders for almost a decade.

As a believer, Frank would often pray for Jim's sobriety and try to encourage him to change. Despite the conversations and the fact that they worked for a Catholic school, Jim's behavior continued to spiral out of control. Frank continued to war in prayer. It was in his heart for the team to come to know Christ and for the kids to grow emotionally, socially, and athletically.

God answered Frank's prayers in a way that was unexpected. Jim was fired despite his winning record. Equally shocking, at least to Frank, is the fact that he was offered the head coaching job. It's clear! God wants nothing or no one to stand in the way of the salvation of souls and the shaping of young minds and hearts. God answered the offensive-based prayers of Frank.

# HOW TO PRAY OFFENSIVE PRAYERS

Where do offensive prayers come from? Three primary sources: God's promises, our passions and goals, and God's revelation. Let's look at each one in turn.

### Pray for God's promises.

God's promises are His pledges to do specific things for you if you live in obedience to His Word. These promises are His vision for your future. They represent His character. He stands behind them 100 percent. They represent God's compassion and care for you. They give you hope and a strategic way to pray. We are even told, "We do not want you to become lazy, but to imitate those who through faith and patience inherit what has been promised" (Heb. 6:12). Since we are to follow the pattern of saints who lived before us, at least in regard to how they pursued God's promises, we cannot overlook the role of prayer in achieving these promises.

Turning over a volume of valuable autographs, Walter Baxendale, an old friend of the famed American evangelist

Dwight L. Moody, said he came across the man's bold, manly signature. Underneath was his favorite text, which he was known to call up in an emergency, taken from Isaiah 50:7: "For the Lord GOD will help me; therefore shall I not be confounded: therefore have I set my face like a flint, and I know that I shall not be ashamed" (KJV). Moody knew the value and success of praying God's promises. God stands behind *all* of His promises. When we pray for these promises to come to pass in our lives, the results are guaranteed. The Scriptures are filled with multiple thousands of promises. Each one has been hand selected by God. Promises represent God's word to you.

When you have no idea of what tomorrow holds or how to pray offensively, find a promise in Scripture and pray it. For example, if you're dealing with chaos at home, on the job, or in a relationship, a wonderful promise to claim in prayer is, "The LORD gives strength to his people; the LORD blesses his people with peace" (Ps. 29:11). This verse tells you that God stands ready, willing, and able to give you—His people— strength and peace. Therefore, when your life is experiencing the opposite or the absence of this promise, you have the right to pray for it.

To wield the weapon of prayer offensively requires that you recognize the gap between where you are and where God wants you to be. Offensive praying can be halted by complacent living. This is why the writer of Hebrews warns us not to become lazy. But rather, we are to diligently mix or integrate our faith and patience with the promises of God. Promises must become real targets toward which we aim our lives and our prayers. As a marksman who shoots his arrow, that is how we should aim our life and prayers. God's promises are worthy targets.

The promises we pray for also fall into the category of protection. For example, Paul says, "No temptation has overtaken you except what is common to mankind. And God is faithful; he will not let you be tempted beyond what you can bear. But when you are tempted, he will also provide a way out so that you can endure it" (1 Cor. 10:13). Since we're in a spiritual war, our adversary's goal is to try to assault us in order to render us unable to fight. His attacks will most likely come in the form of temptations that we succumb to. Praying offensively is to use this 1 Corinthians 10 passage as a prayer guide. It will help us maintain a warrior's alertness against unsuspecting attacks.

On the subject of the value of promises made, a story goes that one day President Abraham Lincoln was riding in a coach with a colonel from Kentucky. The colonel took a bottle of whiskey out of his pocket. He offered Mr. Lincoln a drink. Mr. Lincoln said, "No thank you, Colonel. I never drink whiskey." In a little while the colonel took some cigars out of his pocket and offered one to Mr. Lincoln. Again Mr. Lincoln said, "No, thank you, Colonel." Then Mr. Lincoln said, "I want to tell you a story. One day, when I was about nine years old, my mother called me to her bed. She was very sick. She said, 'Abe, the doctor tells me that I am not going to get well. I want you to be a good boy. I want you to promise me before I go that you will never use whiskey or tobacco as long as you live.' I promised my mother that I never would, and up to this hour, I kept this promise! Would you advise me to break that promise?" The colonel put his hand on Mr. Lincoln's shoulder and said, "Mr. Lincoln, I would not have you break that promise for the world! It is one of the best promises you ever made. I would give a thousand dollars today if I had made my mother a promise like that and had kept it like you have done. I would be a much better man than I am!"[2]

To share another story, the great reformer Martin Luther was a man who enjoyed God's promises because he held the will of God as sacred. In 1540 Frederick Myconius, Luther's close friend and valued assistant, became deathly ill. Expecting to live only a short while longer, he wrote Luther a tender farewell note. As soon as Luther got the note, he shot back this reply: "I command thee in the name of God to live because I still have need of thee in the work of reforming the church.... The Lord will never let me hear that thou art dead, but will permit thee to survive me. For this I am praying, this is my will, and may my will be done, because I seek only to glorify the name of God." Shocking words! But the outcome was that Myconius completely recovered and lived for another six years, outliving Luther by two months.[3]

And speaking of Martin Luther, one of his most popular statements about God's promises is, "When I get hold of a promise…I look upon as I would a fruit tree.… If I would get them I must shake the tree to and fro."[4]

One of the unexpected blessings surrounding promises is that they awaken expectation in us. This expectation shapes our behavior. This truth can be easily seen through a humorous example. After an evening out some parents came home to the children they had left in the care of a babysitter and were pleased to find the kids fast asleep. As the babysitter was about to walk out the door, she said, "By the way, I promised Tommy that if he would stay in bed, you would buy him a pony in the morning." How would you like to be the parent who must now explain to your child, "I'm not going to buy you a pony?" Unlike the babysitter's promise, God's promises are all true. They are not designed to manipulate us to behave in a certain way although we intentionally change our behavior in anticipation of the outcome of the promise.

God's promises are just too powerful to pass up or overlook. If we are observant, we will freely admit: it is God who stirs us to remember or become aware of these very promises. He doesn't want to see us live apart from these wonderful promises. Billy Graham has said, "Heaven is full of answers to prayer for which no one bothered to ask."[5] Could these answers be connected to offensive prayers we never prayed? Prayers that lead the charge into new territory must not be ignored or simply occupy space in our minds. They must be voiced to God. Offensive prayers emerge from promises—God's promises.

### Pray for your passions and goals.

God has wired each of us with aspirations and dreams that drive our thinking, behavior, and goals. We're even wired intuitively to pursue these goals. Paul puts it this way:

> We have different gifts, according to the grace given to each of us. If your gift is prophesying, then prophesy in accordance with your faith; if it is serving, then serve; if it is teaching, then teach; if it is to encourage, then give encouragement; if it is giving, then give generously; if it is to lead, do it diligently; if it is to show mercy, do it cheerfully.
>
> —ROMANS 12:6–8

When we are aware of our wiring and the dreams and passions that can emerge from them, we have a responsibility to pray offensively for their expression. In fact, we must apply true stewardship principles to our lives by setting deliberate targets and goals. Olympic Gold swimmer Michael Phelps said, "At a very young age, I wrote down the goals that I had so I could always see what I wanted to accomplish. And I would look at that goal sheet and think 'I still want to do this.' So I'd decide 'I'm not quitting.'" Just like Phelps directs his daily behavior based on his continued desire to accomplish a long term goal, you must do the same.[6]

We cannot overlook Aristotle's observation: "Man is a goal-seeking animal. His life only has meaning if he is reaching out and striving for his goals."[7] The contribution I add to this statement is that you cannot consider your goals to be noble, important, or valuable if you never pray for their fulfillment and expression. Unfulfilled goals and dreams are like a pregnant woman unable to give birth. Offensive prayers help to bring the vision to term. Offensive prayers help to ensure that the dream is properly and safely birthed.

Offensive prayers are critical to understanding what to do with our passions. Sometimes we cannot figure out our goals. In those instances we need to observe and give expression to our passions. A passion is a desire of the heart, a longing of the soul, a yearning that must be released in order for our true self to be seen. If you don't know or don't have clear goals that can be articulated, then focus on your passions. Then pray that your passions find expression.

The late Earl Nightingale, writer and publisher of inspirational and motivational material, once told a story about a boy named Sparky. For Sparky, school was all but impossible. He failed every subject in the eighth grade. He flunked physics in high school, getting a grade of zero. Sparky also flunked Latin, algebra, and English. He didn't do much better in sports. Throughout his youth Sparky was socially awkward. He wasn't actually disliked by the other students, since no one cared that much. Sparky was a loser. Everyone knew it.

Sparky made up his mind early in life that he would content himself with what appeared to be his inevitable mediocrity. However, one thing was important to Sparky: drawing. He was proud of his artwork. In his senior year of high school, he submitted some cartoons to the editors of the yearbook. The cartoons were turned down. Despite this particular rejection Sparky was so convinced of his ability that he decided to become a professional artist. Later he sent samples of his work to Walt Disney Studios. Once again he was rejected.

Finally Sparky decided to write his own autobiography in cartoons. He described his childhood as a loser and chronic underachiever. And this boy who had such lack of success in school and whose work was rejected again and again was Charles Schulz. He created the world-famous *Peanuts* comic strip, describing himself as the infamously unsuccessful character Charlie Brown. Schulz's innate passion to draw cartoons sought and finally found expression.[8]

Here's another story for you. I have always known Anthony Franklin, my senior associate pastor, to be a man of prayer. Like a pit bull locks his jaw onto something and won't let go, when Anthony locks his heart onto something, he doesn't let go until God's will is accomplished. In May 2009 Anthony's mind became gripped with the idea that his daughter Jessica needed to get on fire for God. He felt this was more than a wishful desire of a father for his eighteen-year-old daughter. This is God's will for every Christ-follower.

Jessica had received Christ as her Savior as a young child. As a preacher's kid, she regularly attended church with her parents and participated in youth groups. Her personal walk with the Lord, however, never demonstrated a burning passion for God. Please don't misunderstand; the character traits of a solid Christian were evident in her life. But the fire for God, the fire that comes from strong seasons of communion with the Lord, was missing.

Anthony's heart was made up. During Jessica's senior year of high school, he was determined to see her heart catch on fire before graduation and the first semester of college. Anthony went on a twenty-eight-day fast. And before the fast was over, God answered his prayer.

Incidentally Jessica knew nothing of her dad's prayer request before God. Since she lived at home, she noticed he wasn't eating but that was nothing uncommon in the Franklin household, as Anthony and Barbara Franklin are praying and fasting people.

During the fast, though, Jessica attended a regional conference called Battle Cry. One evening during the captivating worship experience, Jessica began to cry profusely. She couldn't stop. The tears flowed. It was as if the Holy Spirit was cleaning her heart and washing away all the dryness of soul. Her tears seemed like liquid prayers. Her heart was praying to God without words. Just tears.

From that day forward, Jessica has been on fire for God. She began guarding her daily devotional time with a vengeance. Nothing was going to distract her from daily pursuing God. She started to boldly share her faith with her unsaved friends.

A number of them came to the Lord. When the time came for her to go off to Rutgers University, her faith was stronger than ever. In fact, Jessica became the president of a Christian group on campus. She was also instrumental in leading a number of people to the Lord, her roommate being one of them.

In May 2014 Jessica graduated. As a testament to her devotion to studying, she proudly displays her bachelor of science diploma in business administration. And as a testament to her devotion to Jesus, she proudly maintains her fire for God. None of this would have been possible had prayers not emerged from Anthony's passion.

What could God do with your inborn passions if they were bathed in prayer? God would welcome the opportunity to assist you in finding personal fulfillment with your goals and passions. Prayer is His invitation.

**Pray in response to God's revelation.**

You surely know the story of Jacob, the patriarch of Israel. In one particular part of his story Jacob found himself in an intense spiritual battle borne strictly from his attempt to obey the revelation of God. While working for Laban, his father-in-law, God spoke to Jacob and said, "Go back to the land of your fathers and to your relatives, and I will be with you" (Gen. 31:3). Without questioning, Jacob packed up his family and livestock and headed back to the place of his birth.

Mindful of his moral crimes against his brother Esau twenty-odd years prior, he sent a messenger ahead to send greetings to Esau. In Jewish culture two of the most important things a father can do for his firstborn son is to give him his birthright and a blessing. The birthright included status as head of the family and inheritance of a double portion of the paternal estate. The blessing includes words of encouragement, details concerning the child's inheritance, and prophetic words regarding their future. The lack of blessing was tantamount to a curse.

Through a series of underhanded stunts, Jacob stole both—Esau's birthright and blessing. And Esau had not forgotten Jacob's deceitful behavior. The messenger hastily returned to Jacob with the news that Esau was coming—with four hundred warriors! Their mission was simple: kill Jacob.

What was Jacob to do? He was defenseless. His only solution was to get hold of God. His thinking was, "Certainly God will do something because I'm in His will. I'm in this predicament simply because I am attempting to obey His command to return to the land of my fathers." So Jacob prayed offensively:

> O God of my father Abraham, God of my father Isaac, Lord, you who said to me, "Go back to your country and your relatives, and I will make you prosper," I am unworthy of all the kindness and faithfulness you have shown your servant. I had only my staff when I crossed this Jordan, but now I have become two camps. Save me, I pray, from the hand of my brother Esau, for I am afraid he will come and attack me, and also the mothers with their children. But you have said, "I will surely make you prosper and will make your descendants like the sand of the sea, which cannot be counted."
>
> —Genesis 32:9–12

God was the one who revealed Jacob's future. Because of this, Jacob was able to pray confidently and in faith for a successful outcome to this crisis. Revelation knowledge provides us with that kind of assurance. A revelation is a promise from

God that is not found in the Scripture. It is something God conveys to you through any number of methods. This insight about your future can come through a dream, a prophetic word, a vision, a need, or even a Spirit-directed conversation with another person.

A stimulating conversation can awaken a desire for a certain future reality that had never crossed your mind. This newfound desire leads you into a time of prayer.

This is also what happened to Nehemiah. After his brother, Hanani, shared with him the happenings of Jerusalem, this cup-bearer, who served in the palace of the Babylonian king, could not shake the idea of the need to return to Jerusalem. Nehemiah spent the next few months praying and fasting about his idea. And so Nehemiah returned to Jerusalem with sufficient resources to rebuild the city walls and rehang the gates that had been burned by fire. The city was transformed because this man prayed offensively until God's revelation came to pass.

In a similar way the Lord spoke to my heart many years ago about the need to establish ministry to the whole person. To accomplish that, we needed more space. Our facility at the time was too small, and we'd maximized every square foot of space with innovative practices. The only recourse was to get new space—large space. We found a 107-acre parcel of land with three buildings totaling some 300,000 square feet of space. But the moment we signed contracts and submitted our engineering plans to the local township, an intense public battle began. The battle was so vicious and antagonistic that I had to hire armed bodyguards. The property was zoned for a church, but a handful of detractors began a campaign to try to thwart our reputation and good intentions.

It all came to a head for me one night due to a spiritual dream. In the dream I was in a large meeting room facing the township's planning board. Sitting on my right was my wife, and on my left was the church's chief operating officer. The room was jammed packed with more than a thousand people. They all came with questions, anxiety, and anger. The atmosphere was filled with tension and uncertainty.

Suddenly the officials began to fire questions at me—all kinds of questions, each one trickier and more deceptive than the previous. I noticed, however, that after each of my answers, people got up out of their seats and left the room, as if to say by their departure, "I have no problem with this church." This went on for quite some time. Tricky questions were fired at me; soothing answers were given; people left the room. Finally one of the leaders asked an unusually complicated question—the kind the lawyers used to throw at Jesus in an attempt to trip Him up. By this time there were no more than fifty people in the room. I responded, "I have no answer for your question." A few of the officials turned to one another and whispered.

In the dream I was able to hear what they privately said. They said, "At least we know he's not a liar." At that they all turned to face me. There were no more questions. They were ready to give the official response regarding our application to use the property for our church. One of the officials stood up and said in an authorized tone, "Reverend Ireland, welcome to Rockaway!" Then the dream ended.

This dream, which there was no doubt in my mind was from God, contained a most helpful revelation. It told me that in the natural world, our plans to use this new property as a church campus would be met with great opposition.

At the onset the opposition would be large, but the numbers would drop significantly as my team of professionals and I addressed their questions honestly and respectfully. I was to patiently stay the course.

The revelation also gave me an understanding of how to offensively pray. I knew what God desired for the outcome. This emboldened me.

Although this dream provided a heavenly glimpse of a forthcoming earthly reality, the live performance was still stressful and difficult. The actual battle lasted three-and-a-half years publicly and privately. The first meeting with the planning board had to be held in a regional high school because there were about sixteen hundred people in attendance. There were more than a dozen police officers stationed around the perimeter of the room. It was that contentious, as I had seen in my dream.

Throughout the duration of the public battle, the number of people in the audience dropped each month we met. At the final public hearing, three-and-a-half years from the first hearing, there were fewer than fifty people in the small municipal meeting room. This was exactly what was revealed to me in my dreams years prior! And we received a favorable vote that evening.

As I was leaving the municipal building that night, flanked by my two armed bodyguards, the township's chief of police walked me to my car. Immediately before I got into my vehicle, he said to me in an official tone, "Reverend Ireland, welcome to Rockaway!" Instantly my mind went back to the scene in my dream almost four years before that forecasted this statement that sealed the favorable outcome. I turned to him and said, "Thank you." Then I drove off knowing

God had galvanized a principle in my mind—that offensive prayers emerge from God's revelation! We have a responsibility to pray about God's revelations regardless of the route they take to get to us.

## GOD IS ALWAYS PREVIOUS!

The Austrian theologian Friedrich von Hügel said, "God is always previous."[9] This means that we can never take pride in coming up with an offensive prayer apart from God's promptings. In His infinite wisdom God allows us to get a glimpse of a future goal or a desired outcome. The revelation is so inviting that we begin to pray offensively for it to be fulfilled.

This is what God did with Daniel. Scripture declares, "In the third year of Cyrus king of Persia, a revelation was given to Daniel...and it concerned a great war" (Dan. 10:1). Captivated by the vision from God, the prophet entered a twenty-one-day period of fasting and prayer. The vision caused Daniel to be forward-looking with his prayers. God needed someone to pray offensively about His desired future for the world. Daniel made himself available.

Since God is always previous, I encourage you to periodically pray: "God, show me what You want me to pray about. Reveal to me Your plans for my generation so that I can start praying toward that end." Praying this way demonstrates a growing maturity on your part. It also aligns you with the *partnership* heart of God. God welcomes partnerships. In fact, we're told: "Surely the Sovereign LORD does nothing without revealing his plan to his servants the prophets" (Amos 3:7). As a servant of the Lord, I'm going to run with this open invitation to team up with God. From this passage I learn that

God is always at work around me. And because of His collaborative nature, He invites me into His work. Therefore, I cannot simply live a defensive life. I must be offensive in my lifestyle and prayers.

Start praying offensively! It is the will of God!

*Chapter 8*

# WHAT'S YOUR RANK, SOLDIER?

A FARMER ONCE TOOK an eagle egg and placed it in his hen's nest, so the eagle was raised with chickens. Try as he might, the young eagle always had trouble trying to be a chicken. His heart kept telling him something wasn't right. Much of the time he was lonely because he didn't fit in. One day he tried to take flight by flapping his wings and the farmer caught him and clipped his wings. This eagle would look up to the sky, knowing deep in his soul he belonged up among the clouds. Weeks passed, when all of a sudden a storm came, sending all the scared chickens running for cover. But the little eagle was not afraid. He faced the storm. It had been some time since the farmer had clipped the eagle's wings. His feathers had grown back. He flapped his wings and was able to take off. Soon he was out of the chicken yard forever.

I like this story because it tells us that we can break free from anything that is holding us back from being what God intended us to be. God has a purpose for you, and He doesn't want you to stay in the barnyard. I am not saying it's easy. It will take hard work. You'll need to take risks, endure loneliness, leave some things behind, make hard decisions, risk being misunderstood, and likely be judged and criticized before you enjoy the fullness of God in your life. But just as the eagle was uncomfortable in a chicken yard, you too will be unhappy if you do not seek to fulfill your calling. Your hunger to be more than you are is a God-given hunger found only with life in Him.

The primary reason why the eagle longed to soar high in the sky was because it was created to do that. Its ambition was to fulfill its divinely inspired purpose. The eagle's aspiration was not to bring attention to itself. Rather, it was to bring attention to the magnificence of its Creator—the Lord Almighty. Similarly our ambition must be divinely linked to the honor of God. Anything less than that will create a self-centered approach to life and prayer. Ambition provides direction to my prayers.

## AMBITION OPENS THE DOOR FOR POTENTIAL

As Christians, we have demonized ambition. Ambition is an eager or strong desire to achieve something. It is a powerful internal driving force that feeds one's potential. Nowhere in Scripture are we told to not have it. In fact, the Scripture teaches just the opposite. Paul said to young Timothy, "Here is a trustworthy saying: Whoever aspires to be an overseer desires a noble task" (1 Tim. 3:1). An overseer is an elder or a pastor. This highly esteemed role in the Lord's church is a significant and honorable one. Yet Paul doesn't warn, scold, or object to someone having ambition for that or *any* office. The verses that follow simply outline the character requirements necessary to hold such an office.

From Paul's counsel to Timothy, we learn that having ambition is not bad. We must temper it, however, so we don't run ahead of God, become self-absorbed, or grow full of pride. To temper my ambition, I am guided by the motto: "I must *live* facing Jesus; *walk* with sensitivity to the Holy Spirit; and have a *deepening* dependence on God." This threefold practice keeps me grounded without compromising my God-given potential.

I am free to pursue my potential without winding up in the spiritual graveyard where many ambitious people end up because they lacked moral and ethical guidelines. Too much ambition—or better put, ambition without proper boundaries—is wrong. And equally wrong is having no ambition at all. This is why Mark Twain pointed out, "Keep away from people who try to belittle your ambitions. Small people always do that, but the really great make you feel that you, too, can become great."[1] Recognizing the value of reaching our potential, Ralph Waldo Emerson said, "What I need is someone who will make me do what I can."[2] I challenge you to frame this statement into a prayer that you'll pray often.

## YOU NEED MORE THAN JUST PURPOSE

Many people pray and fast to understand their purpose. That's commendable. The problem is that once they know their God-ordained purpose, they often settle in and relax. To them, they're being obedient in fulfilling their purpose as a soldier in God's army. "Certainly that must be good enough," they think. Little do they know that our General has plans for their ongoing growth and development! It would be a disservice to you *and* the army for you to not fulfill your potential. Prayer gives you access to your potential!

To further the point, take this story of legendary baseball catcher Yogi Berra, who was in a tie game with two outs in the bottom of the ninth. The player from the opposing team stepped up to bat and made the sign of the cross on home plate with his bat. Berra was a Catholic too, but he wiped off the plate with his glove and said to the batter, "Why don't we let God just watch this game?"[3] That is good theology when it comes to a baseball game. However, it's not how you should approach the discovery of your potential. Don't just let God watch. Pray strategically for His help to unlock your destiny.

Although prayer is crucial to defining your future, it is not the only factor. God looks at the whole person when considering them for a promotion. He looks at our character, faithfulness, ability to properly represent Him, and scores of other important measures, such as our stewardship practices. *Stewardship* is a big umbrella term that signifies our acknowledgement of God as the owner of everything and ourselves as managers. Our advancement is based on how effectively we steward God's resources under our care. God has the right to promote us as He sees fit. Yet we must not overlook our responsibility to be ready in prayer for whatever task our General requires of us. In prayer our hearts are readied for every battle. In prayer our hearts are awakened and prepared to seize opportunities that lead to the fulfillment of our potential.

## SOLDIERS HAVE POTENTIAL

That we are soldiers in the army of the Lord is foundational knowledge to most believers. We get that. We often pay too little attention to the need to fulfill our *potential* as soldiers.

Here we find that the weapon of prayer is not just a tool we use to thwart our dark adversary. It is a key that is to be used to unlock our purpose and our potential. Prayer gives us access to the General. Since God is the consummate strategist, the perfect tactician, and the finest forward thinker, you cannot be in His war room for long without learning His purpose for your life: life in His army. Generals recognize the gifting of their officers and assign them accordingly.

At the heels of Paul's conversion, for example, he spent three consecutive days and nights in prayer and fasting. He had to figure out his spiritual assignment. For what purpose did Christ save him? It was more than being rescued from hell. That was Paul's prize—a most important one. But what was on the General's heart for Paul? What was Paul saved for? That piece of information was revealed through a disciple named Ananias at the end of Paul's three days with the General. The Scripture reports:

> But the Lord said to Ananias, "Go! This man [Paul] is my instrument to proclaim my name to the Gentiles and their kings and to the people of Israel. I will show him how much he must suffer for my name."
> —ACTS 9:15–16

Paul was to be a messenger—a preacher proclaiming the message of God's love before the Gentiles. The purpose was clear. But what was Paul's potential? Generals also recognize the potential of their officers and stretch them accordingly.

To clarify, *potential* answers a different question than *purpose*. Purpose speaks of intent and direction, while potential deals with scope and capacity. I'm sure you've heard it said about someone, "He could do so much more!" The phrase is directed at wasted potential. There still remains more height, breadth, and level of influence than what meets the eye.

In this and other extended times of prayer and fasting, Paul was able to have the General unlock his potential. Ananias's revelation said that Paul would speak before Gentiles "and their kings and before the people of Israel." In other words, Paul's potential went well beyond addressing the rank and file among the Gentiles. He was to stand before their decision makers and earthly pontiffs. His sphere of influence would also reach the Jews. He had the potential to be a cross-cultural ambassador of the kingdom of God.

Remember again Nehemiah, the Old Testament Jewish cup-bearer who poured wine for the Babylonian king, Artaxerxes. The cupbearer's role was menial. His primary duty was to taste the wine before the king drank it. This was to ensure that the pitcher of wine had not been poisoned by one of the king's enemies. Although Nehemiah faithfully attended in this position of servitude, he had untapped potential. It all came to a head following the visit of an international guest—Hanani (Neh. 1:1–4). Hanani shared with Nehemiah the problems going on back home in Jerusalem. Deep concern for the physical and emotional needs of his people filled Nehemiah's heart.

He couldn't shake the idea that something must be done. Rather than settle for a passive feeling of empathy for the demoralized Jews, he turned his anguish into a lengthy season of prayer and fasting. Based on the timetable in the text—the month *Kislev* (November/December) through the month *Nisan* (March/April)—we learn that this man spent approximately five to six months praying and fasting. He was spending time with the General.

Like Paul, Nehemiah's purpose and potential were unlocked. His burden for Jerusalem and its people was not a fleeting one. He knew that God had purposed him to bring change and healing to this great city and its people. Through prayer, he realized that his base role of cupbearer gave him an entrée to the powerful king. He skillfully leveraged his role to gain access to the king's authorization and resources (Neh. 2:1–9).

None of Nehemiah's requests were selfish in nature. He was strictly operating as an advocate for the demoralized people back home. There is no doubt that Nehemiah's time in prayer resulted in tremendous favor from the king. When he goes to Jerusalem, he organizes the city leaders, provides a plan to rebuild the broken walls of the city, and completes the project even in the face of outside agitators. In another impressive feat Nehemiah challenged the Jews and priests alike to return to God and the ways of their fathers.

None of this would have happened if Nehemiah hadn't allowed God to challenge him to fulfill his potential. Imagine that: a cupbearer becoming a city builder! And the process started in prayer. Prior to that Nehemiah wasn't even praying about his potential, untapped or recognized. When his soul became burdened for his people, he chose to get hold of God in prayer. Once he got hold of God, he allowed God the General to get hold of him—His soldier.

What would happen if you decided to do the same thing? What would your world look like if you used the key of prayer to unlock the door to your potential?

## RECOGNIZE YOUR POTENTIAL

Have you ever seen the Geico commercial where a father and son are hanging out and the son's playing video games while the father is using his tablet? The father says, "Huh. Fifteen minutes could save you 15 percent or more on car insurance." The son replies, "Everybody knows that." Then the dad says, "Well, did you know that Pinocchio was a bad motivational speaker?" The commercial quickly cuts to a lecture hall where Pinocchio is giving a motivational speech to an audience of business people. He says, "I look around this room, and I see nothing but untapped potential." Pinocchio then points to a man in the crowd and confidently says, "You have potential!" Immediately Pinocchio's nose starts to grow. The man identified in the crowd is as familiar with the fairy tale as everyone else. As Pinocchio's nose grows because he's lying, the man bows his head sadly, depressed that even a motivational speaker doesn't believe he has much to offer.[4]

Fortunately you don't have to attend a motivational workshop to learn of your untapped potential. There are two sure-fire ways to discover it. First, when something internal in you cries out for expression, fulfillment, or attention, and second, when something external to you keeps calling you.

**Notice the internal voices.**

Vision, goals, and dreams are things deep within your heart that cry for fulfilment. Your potential is understood when you answer these questions: What do you keep imagining, day-dreaming, or talking about? What would you do if you didn't care what others thought? Or if you weren't afraid? Here's another question that helps you identify the internal longings of your soul, the place where potential lies: What excites you? Answer this question, and you've located your passion.

It will certainly require hard work and much focus in prayer to realize your dreams and God-given potential. But this is worthy of your attention anyway. These objectives that originate from within can also serve the unmet societal needs.

Take the example of William Booth, the founder of the Salvation Army. He was returning home late at night in December 1887, and his cab had just crossed London Bridge. As he looked through the window, he saw a sight that shocked him—what appeared to be about twenty men huddled together for warmth under the bridge. That night he couldn't sleep because what he witnessed gave him no peace. The next morning when Bramwell, his adult son, and a member of the Salvation Army was visiting, William shared what he had witnessed under the bridge the night before.

Bramwell said he knew about the tragedy but concluded that the Salvation Army couldn't help. General Booth sighed deeply and said to his son, "But, Bramwell, there are still men sleeping out in the winter under the bridges. Do something, Bramwell! Do something! Something must be done." Shortly thereafter the Salvation Army was able to secure a warehouse and provide beds and hot meals for the men because once people had the vision painted for them, they supported it financially.[5]

Without taking anything away from Bramwell, it is clear that General Booth was the one who became burdened by the sight of the needy men. It was his vision that was in need of being fulfilled. God had troubled his heart. His untapped potential was being identified.

Similarly when God stirs your heart, others close to you or even in your family may not be stirred. And it is not to be a source of contention or an indictment against their indifference toward social responsibility, if that happens. It may very well be indicative that God is stirring you, not them, to do something about what you feel deep down inside.

**Notice the external cues.**

Second, your potential is unfulfilled when something external keeps calling you. If you're intrigued or challenged by something someone else has accomplished, this may be an indication that you too are called to do something similar.

For example, in May 1954 Roger Bannister broke the world record and ran a mile in under four minutes. In the whole of human history no one had been able to do that. Prior to this event it was considered impossible—beyond the physical limits of the human body. Year after year runners had come closer and closer, but no one was able to break the four-minute barrier.

Not only did Bannister practice and train hard, but he also constantly rehearsed the event in his mind until he truly believed that he could do it, even though it had never been done. Yet within six weeks of Bannister breaking this psychological barrier, it was broken again, and within a few years the mile had been run in under four minutes hundreds of times![6] Belief holds us back more than anything else—far more than fear. More, even, than physical constraints.

If you have an ache inside your soul to accomplish something, don't be deterred because no one else has done it. Consider sixty-four-year-old Diana Nyad, the endurance swimmer who swam from Cuba to Florida in September 2013. She's the first person to complete this mind-numbing feat. Without a shark cage, she swam one hundred ten miles in fifty-three consecutive hours. This was her fifth attempt. She tried once in 1978 and three times between 2011 and 2012. Though the first four attempts were unsuccessful, she could not shake the goal. She went through the arduous training, psyching herself up to the task, formulating a good support team, and then taking the plunge—literally.[7]

Bannister and Nyad were driven to pursue their goals and potential. They were both successful. What would happen if you put in the same level of hard work toward the goals you know God has assigned you to champion? What would happen if you added something even more potent to that hard work?

Add prayer! Prayer is a game-changer because it invites partnership with God. As we learned from examining a small portion of Nehemiah's life, prayer was instrumental in unlocking his potential.

In the book *The Billy Graham Story* we learn that Dr. Graham's purpose became crystal clear one night in March 1938 as a result of prayer. He says, "I remember getting on my knees and saying, 'O God, if you want me to preach, I will do it.'" Soon afterward God also revealed to him his potential. Graham walks us down memory lane when he recounts, "'I used to walk those empty streets in Temple Terrace praying. I would pray sometimes three or four hours at a stretch. And then,' he recalled a quarter of a century after, 'in the most unusual way I used to have the strangest glimpses of these great crowds that I now preach to....I think I saw myself as participating in some way in what Billy Sunday and D. L. Moody had witnessed—big stadiums, big meetings.'"[8] Prayer unlocked his purpose and his potential. It will do the same for you and me.

## THE VALUE OF LISTENING PRAYER

Stories such as Billy Graham's always boost my faith. They remind me that when I draw near to God, He will thrust me far into my potential. He did the same to Paul and Barnabas after they spent focused time in worship, prayer, and fasting. As pastors of the church at Antioch alongside Simeon, Lucius, and Manaen, these five men knew the value and the priority of prayer. The account reads, "While they were worshiping the Lord and fasting, the Holy Spirit said, 'Set apart for me Barnabas and Saul for the work to which I have called them.' So after they had fasted and prayed, they placed their hands on them and sent them off" (Acts 13:2–3).

The role of a pastor is not an easy one. You're constantly giving out in order to provide care, counsel, direction, and, at times, correction to the congregation. If you don't make time to recharge and refuel, as with any profession, you'll soon face burnout. And if you don't spend special times in prayer and fasting, you'll never take new territory for Christ. Without these prayer retreats, your ministry will face a decline or at best a standstill, never an advance.

Offensive praying is a large part of such prayer retreats. In this instance these pastors wanted to advance the mission and strength of the church at Antioch. They also wanted to see a marked improvement in the effectiveness of their individual and team leadership performances. These are the kinds of topics pastors pray about while on retreats. Whatever topics they present before the Lord, they are resolved on this fact: prayer is the key to victory.

Since prayer is a dialogue, a significant amount of your private time should be spent listening for the Lord's response. When you quiet your heart and mind from the pressures you face and the many decisions still requiring your input, instead of simply meditating on God, you're listening. Listening prayers start the moment you begin expecting God to speak. God is a person with feelings, longings, ideas, and thoughts, and He is willing to communicate them. He wants to say something to you. When you believe that, you prepare your heart to listen for His voice.

Listening prayer means that you give God an opportunity to speak. Don't limit your prayers to declarations, closed-end statements, and conclusions. Pose questions. Ask for clarity. Request insight and wisdom in the matters you're praying about. In other words, create a platform for God to speak into. Often our prayers are spoken in a matter-of-fact manner even though we are seeking advice and input from the Almighty. We've all been guilty of this method of prayer at one time or another. It's now time to change permanently. Let your prayers have a healthy mix of statements *and* questions. This makes for a good conversation—a dialogue where God can speak into things while you listen quietly.

As the pastors listened that day, suddenly a prophetic word punctured the quietness of the room. God spoke. He said, "Set apart for me Barnabas and Saul for the work to which I have called them" (v. 2). The word held a clear message regarding the future. The two founding pastors, Paul and Barnabas, were to transition their relationship with the Antioch church. They were no longer going to serve that congregation in a full-time stationary capacity. Rather, that church would become a home base from which they would serve the world.

The prophetic word contained their call to apostolic ministry. God was commissioning them to develop leaders and plant independent congregations in other parts of the world. Periodically they would return home to Antioch to rest, recharge, and reconnect, but their mission was to go to the world. This mission captured their potential. And it was during their time of prayer that their potential was awakened and communicated.

I'm sure it was a hard decision for Paul and Barnabas to redefine their roles at the church at Antioch. An even more painful undertaking was to share the news with the flock. Can you just picture that conversation? "God has called Paul and Barnabas to the world. They will not be with us on a permanent basis, as they have been since our inception." I'm sure the congregation had mixed feelings, as did Paul and Barnabas. This was going to be a new undertaking. But since the orders were given by their General, He also provided the grace to carry it out.

What would have happened if Paul and Barnabas had not pressed into God in prayer? Would they have delayed the receipt of their orders? Or better yet, would they have become satisfied in being local church pastors? Only God knows the answers to these and similar questions. The one thing that can be understood from their time of protracted prayer is this: their potential was not going to be fulfilled if they remained in Antioch. As soldiers in God's army, their rank was greater than their current assignment and function. The General had to give them an assignment that matched their potential.

## TAP IN TO YOUR POTENTIAL

There are many things in our lives we cannot control. One thing we can control, though, is how we deal with problems and unwanted circumstances. Certainly our attitude is our responsibility to adjust and control. Our commitment to prayer is something else that falls under our control.

Problems should not drive us to behave in ways contrary to our faith. Problems should not cause our prayer life to become nonexistent. If they do, we are limiting our growth and our potential for promotion in God's army.

Two of the big goals we as Christians aim for are to become like Christ and to introduce Christ to others. We aim to become like Christ in our behavior, values, worldview, and submission to God. We introduce others to Christ by fulfilling the Great Commission. Both of these goals include making a full commitment to being a conduit of God's power through the Holy Spirit. This will result in people living the God kind of life within our sphere of influence. To accomplish either of these goals requires prayer. Again we see that prayer is the backbone of the Christian.

Our potential for promotion in the army of the Lord is tied to our success in achieving these two goals. This statement can be stated in a slightly different way without taking away from its accuracy: our potential for promotion is based on our successes in prayer. Not only does prayer awaken our potential, but it also brings us the victory we're seeking. That victory leads us to pursue other victories through the weapon of prayer.

I'll share with you a story to illustrate. Our church typically begins the New Year with a twenty-one-day Daniel fast. This particular fast, taken from the Book of Daniel, calls for eating a plant-based diet and drinking water in lieu of fruit juices or other types of beverages. Several thousand people commit to it as a means of drawing closer to the Lord and achieving some needed breakthrough in their lives.

Chris and Tara, a young couple in South Jersey, learned about our Daniel fast from his in-laws, and Chris was on board even though he was a member of another church. He wanted to enter 2014 with a closer relationship with Christ and a stronger anointing upon his life. He felt that somehow he was underused by God and pressing into God through prayer would correct that. He was also particularly burdened for his fifteen-year-old son, Bryce.

Bryce was a good kid. Although he knew Christ, his faith had been shaken to the core by some of the topics being taught in his science class. Subjects such as evolution made him quite skeptical of God, the Bible, and the Christian faith. His cynicism and skepticism were becoming an area of great concern to his parents. Talk was not helping. They decided to make Bryce's spiritual condition the major focal point of their fast.

As Chris drove Bryce to school one morning, he said to him, "God is going to have to blow your mind!" What Chris meant was that a dramatic encounter with God was the only way Bryce's skepticism was going to be reversed. It needed to be undeniable. It needed to be unexplainable through human reasoning. It needed to be a God thing. The words were almost prophetic.

A week or so before the fast Bryce went to see the horror movie *Paranormal Activity: The Marked Ones*. It featured a teenage boy who received paranormal power from contact with the dark world of witchcraft and satanic activities. Bryce found it so disturbing that within the first ten minutes of the show, he walked out of the theater. As he was leaving, he felt something blow across his face. He thought nothing of it.

That very week Bryce began to have trouble sleeping. He started having nightmares, hearing voices in his head, and became very paranoid and anxious. He began complaining to his family about his insomnia and the feeling of walking around in a daze.

By this time Chris and Tara had begun fasting and praying for Bryce to have a dramatic encounter with God that would lead to his deliverance. It all came to a head one evening when Chris recognized through prayer that a demonic spirit was oppressing his son. As he walked into Bryce's room, Bryce began to cry uncontrollably. This was most unusual for Bryce. Immediately the dark spirit spoke through him, saying, "Why do you have to pray? Why do you have to fast?"

Apparently his parents' fasting and praying had agitated the demonic spirit, and it was annoyed. From annoyance, the mood shifted to fear because these words came next: "Get away from me; I'm afraid of you!" Bryce began to look at Chris with fear in his eyes. It was an unnatural kind of fear—the kind of fear when a lesser power is confronted by a greater one. The unclean spirit was uncovered and was about to be exorcised by the power of the Holy Spirit as in the days of Jesus.

As Chris was recounting the story to me, he said, "A supernatural boldness came over me, and I knew that God was going to free my son from this demonic bondage." Chris began to speak sternly to the demonic force, saying that he had no authority to harass his son. He said, "In the name of Jesus, I charge you to leave Bryce now!"

Immediately Bryce was set free. Fear left his eyes. Peace flooded his soul. He was freed from the torment.

Intuitively Chris asked, "Son, do you want to recommit your life to Christ?" Without any hesitation, Bryce surrendered his heart to the Lord. His whole face smiled the moment he ended the short prayer of rededication. He reasserted that Christ was his Savior. All of his arguments, skepticism, and uncertainties about God and the need for a personal Savior were dismissed. Bryce was so confident of his newfound faith that he wrote down in his journal, "On January 16, 2014, I gave my life to Christ." The encounter was so dramatic that he excitedly blurted out, "I just want to tell all my friends about Jesus! I feel clean, washed, and set free." There was no question that Chris and Tara's prayers were answered. God blew Bryce's mind.

Chris's other prayer was also answered. He felt that God opened a new dimension of Himself to Chris. The idea of helping others find freedom in Christ was no longer Bible stories far removed from his life. He too was being used as a soldier in the army of the Lord. Through prayer, his untapped potential was awakened. Chris found the pathway to promotion: prayer.

If a soldier effectively uses the weapon of prayer to win battles, wouldn't you consider this soldier for promotion? I would. And if through the weapon of prayer a soldier gains freedom and deliverance for others, wouldn't you look to promote that soldier? I certainly would. Just as Chris did, if you pursue the deliverance of others, victory will position you for promotion and increase of your rank in the army of the Lord.

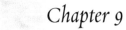

*Chapter 9*

# THE MOUNTAIN
# OF THE LORD

OVER THE PAST decade I've become an avid runner. At first it was to drop weight. That happened! Now it's because I can't live without it. I even participate in local races just for fun. I enjoy it.

But when I was in Kenya for a recent speaking engagement, I donned my gear early one morning and headed out. A couple of miles in I couldn't help but notice the many stares and strange looks from the Kenyans I passed. I almost became self-conscious. Was it my outfit? Was it my form? Yet I knew neither was the case. Some people run with this weird form, as if a dog is chasing them or they're dancing or skipping. I knew that wasn't me because my running buddy back home would have said something. I thought long and hard as I continued on my run. What could it be? Why all the stares?

At breakfast I asked one of my Kenyan hosts. I'll never forget his response. He said, "Real athletes train in the mountains! The people are shocked to see you training here in the lower elevations." To give you context, I was visiting Nakuru, a village three hours north of Kenya's capital, Nairobi. The elevation in Nakuru is approximately 5,800 feet above sea level. This elevation may seem high to you and was certainly high to me since Rockaway, New Jersey, is about 550 feet above sea level. I was huffing and puffing the whole time because my body wasn't used to that elevation! But to the Kenyans I wasn't a serious runner; in their thinking, if you're not serious, why run at all.

One of the main training hubs in Kenya is situated atop the Rift Valley, a location some 8,000 feet above sea level. No wonder Kenyans are world renowned long-distance runners! Read off the names of the first five runners to cross the finish line in most marathons and invariably at least one Kenyan is on that list. What my host was saying to me in a kind manner was, "If you want to have real success with running, you must go to the mountains."

## LET'S GO TO THE MOUNTAIN!

The same things holds true spiritually. If you want to have real success in your prayer life, you must go to the mountain of the Lord. The prophet Isaiah declared:

> In the last days the mountain of the LORD's temple will be established as the highest of the mountains; it will be exalted above the hills, and all nations will stream to it. Many peoples will come and say, "Come, let us go up to the mountain of the LORD, to the temple of the God of Jacob."
>
> —ISAIAH 2:2–3

The phrases *mountain of the Lord* and *mountain of God* appear some fourteen times in the Bible. Historically, and as Isaiah prophesied in his day, people met with God on mountaintops. Sometimes God invited them. Other times they voluntarily chose to ascend the mountain to meet with God.

It all started with Abraham. God gave the invitation: "Take your son, your only son, whom you love—Isaac—and go to the region of Moriah. Sacrifice him there as a burnt offering on a mountain I will show you" (Gen. 22:2). Abraham obeyed. As he was about to sacrifice Isaac, God intervened. He passed God's test. God wanted to know if Abraham loved Him more than his son Isaac. Instead of sacrificing Isaac, God allowed Abraham to discover a ram caught by its horn in a nearby bush. That was to be his sacrifice. In response, "Abraham called that place The LORD Will Provide. And to this day it is said, 'On the mountain of the LORD it will be provided'" (v. 14).

Believers have come to enjoy worshipping God on mountaintops because it symbolizes a place of provision. Ascending the mountain would give the worshipper private time with God. In the case of Abraham, God was calling him away from life's busyness. This time on the mountain was designed to pull him away from the mundane, from the routine. As Abraham climbed the mountain, it symbolized his making an ascent to God. We human beings tend to envision that God is seated at a high place in the heavens. The journey up the mountainside allowed Abraham and Isaac to journey away from where people lived, socialized, and conducted their affairs toward where God lived instead.

Once atop the mountain Abraham met with God. His love for God was proven, and his need to replace Isaac with an animal sacrifice was provided. From Abraham's declaration, "On the mountain of the LORD it will be provided," we conclude that our needs will be provided for on the mountain of the Lord. This is why the mountain of the Lord—a symbolic place—is so captivating.

Natural mountains are alluring, seductive, and mesmerizing. These majestic alps are inviting and welcoming. It's almost as if a mountain calls out to you: *"Climb me! Come here!"*

On a recent visit to Colorado Springs, I stayed at Glen Eyrie, a grand and historic property built by the city's founder. This is an English Tudor-style castle owned by the Navigators and is situated near the northwest foothills of the Colorado mountains. Tucked away on this gorgeous, eight hundred-acre piece of property, this hotel recognizes its beauty and the alluring qualities associated with the views it offers. From the grounds you see the majestic mountains reaching up toward the sky. Each peak looks more inviting than the next. In an almost hypnotic sense the mountain peaks call out to onlookers: "Come and climb me. Come closer. Check me out!" To bring soberness to incoming guests, we were required to sign a waiver. The hotel takes no legal responsibility and warns against your climbing the nearby mountains. I'm a city lover, yet admittedly, the mountains did look tempting. I signed the waiver.

Even so, the mountain of the Lord is more captivating and alluring than natural mountains. According to Isaiah's prophecy the mountain of the Lord will become more established than ever in the last days. Its captivating quality will become increasingly fascinating to people of every nation as we near the last days. And people will stream to it and invite others to "go up to the mountain of the Lord."

This is what I'm doing right now. I'm inviting you to go to the mountain of the Lord. There are three main reasons why you should go:

1. To meet with God

2. To find relief

3. To receive your rewards

## GO TO MEET WITH GOD

On the subject of going to the mountain to meet with God, I was privileged to pick the brain of an old minister when I was in my late twenties. I asked him, "What do you regret the most in all your years of ministry?" He pondered my question and gave this thoughtful response: "I regret not spending more time in pursuit of God. I struggle to go away and simply seek God." His words have grown to have more and more value to me over the years. Now that I'm entering my fourth decade of ministry, the old man's regret has become my regret. If I don't intentionally block out time in my calendar to meet with God, it won't happen. I'm not talking about standard daily devotions. I mean the need to carve out a few days where you go away or shut-in for the sole purpose of meeting with God. Every time I've done it, something special and life transforming always occurs. You cannot meet with God and leave unchanged. That's impossible!

A few years ago I came up with a personal plan to meet with God regularly. I take two days bimonthly to go to the mountain of the Lord. These spiritual retreats occur in tranquil, serene places where I can pray, read Scripture, and commune with God without a hint of distraction. On the rare times when I can't get away, I lock in at my home. Choosing to meet with God must be intentional! There is never a good time to get away; the same way there's never a good time to start a diet, to get sick, or to have a tooth pulled.

Over time I began to recognize the correlation between my times with God and my effectiveness in ministry. Regular seasons on the mountaintop enlarged my faith, deepened my dependency on God, and increased my expectation for God to set people free through my ministry. One of those trophies was Ray.

Ray, someone who had become disconnected from God, was determined to get back on track spiritually. At nine years old he received personal ministry at church from a visiting evangelist. The guest minister spotted Ray in the crowd and asked him to come forward. The boy stepped out of the crowd and into the spotlight of the altar area. The evangelist gave him a prophetic word to the effect of: "You will be a fiery preacher for God. Your ministry will be that of an evangelist. You will not preach for financial gain but out of a love for God and His people." Ray fed on that word for years.

When he became an adult, however, he found himself in a backslidden state. His pursuit of career, family, and things that occupy the minds of most people had taken over Ray's heart. He languished in this spiritually barren and dry place for roughly ten years. Then one day his mind started to drift back to childhood days, days that had fond memories of a once beautiful relationship with God. He decided to make the long walk back to serving God in fervency and deep devotion. Ray had missed God. He'd missed spending time with God. He'd missed sensing the presence of God.

One Bible promise that Ray knew and began to apply was, "You will seek me and find me when you seek me with all your heart" (Jer. 29:13). So Ray began to pray and fast regularly in the hope of rebuilding his relationship with God. To his surprise, the road back was not far at all. One Sunday he found himself at our church. We had a visiting minister. As chance would have it, the minister called Ray out of the audience and prophesied to him the exact same words the evangelist did in his mother's church when he was nine years old! It was as if God was saying to Ray, "I have not changed My mind about you." Today Ray is on my staff, and one of his duties is to lead the men's ministry. As a fiery preacher, he helps men maximize their manhood.

**Come hungry and thirsty.**

I've discovered over the years that believers who hunger and thirst for God are the ones who tend to carve out time to meet with Him. *Hunger* and *thirst* are two metaphors that we all can understand. Throughout Scripture they are used to describe those who are utterly desperate to get to the next spiritual level. They are insanely eager to serve God's purpose, which includes adjusting their lives to increasingly please God.

Here's a real-life example to help make my point. In Kano, Nigeria, I remember being physically parched when I was headed to the airport. The daytime temperature was about 120 degrees Fahrenheit. It was hot to say the least. The car had no air-conditioning. One thing I recall from my engineering days was glass is an insulator of heat. Heat goes out at a slower rate than it enters through the windshield. This made the temperature inside the car feel at least 10 degrees hotter than outside. I was literally burning up. When I finally got a chance to catch my breath from the three-hour drive and going through the ordeal of customs, it dawned on me: "I'm really thirsty." This was not a normal type of thirstiness. I never felt like this before. I knew instinctually that I must be dehydrated.

It was too late, however, to purchase a bottle of water. As we sat on the runway preparing to fly to Egypt, all I could do was think about how thirsty I was. I sat there impatiently waiting for the flight attendant to make her rounds with the snack cart. When she finally came, I received a small glass of water. It looked like a shot glass. I mean, all the glass had was just one little swallow. I asked for another hit of water. She didn't understand me because of the language barrier; she only spoke Arabic, and I only spoke English. So I held out the little shot glass with a pitiful look on my face. She understood. I needed more water. She filled the little shot glass and walked away. Again, I downed it in an instant. My thirst was still unquenched.

When she came back around the third time, I made some gestures to indicate, "Please give me the entire two-liter bottle in your hand." She figured out what was going on. She smiled as she handed me the bottle. I drank until I was refueled.

This is what God wants each of us to do. We must admit our thirstiness and then drink—and keep on drinking until we are full!

## Come connect with God.

On the mountaintop your soul feeds on God. You connect with Him. He shapes your values, your priorities, and your person. On the mountaintop you fall more deeply in love with Him. In the classic book *The Pursuit of God* A. W. Tozer wrote, "Come near to the holy men and women of the past and you will soon feel the heat of their desire after God. They mourned for Him, they pray and wrestled and sought for Him day and night, in season and out, and when they had found Him the finding was all the sweeter for the long seeking."[1] What made these men and women leave their marks on history is the fact that they were seekers after God for their generations. Every generation needs thirsty men and women who will cry, "Let us go to the mountain of the Lord!"

Sometimes when you go to the mountain of the Lord, your sole objective is to connect with God. You don't want anything but time with Him. You're not asking for money. You're not asking for help with your problems. There are times for that. Your primary request is to simply meet with Him. You're hungry for God. You're thirsty for Him. Your soul is on a "God diet." He's your meal—your only meal!

Moses had many such visits. The most significant one— the one that led to him receiving the Ten Commandments— went like this: "When Moses went up on the mountain, the cloud covered it, and the glory of the LORD settled on Mount Sinai. For six days the cloud covered the mountain, and on the seventh day the LORD called to Moses from within the cloud" (Exod. 24:15–16). Imagine that. For six days there was nothing but silence on Moses's part and on God's part. Neither needed to talk. They were doing what they both wanted to do, what both longed to do, what brought both of them pleasure. They were spending time with each other. Moses wanted to meet with God, and God also wanted to meet with Moses. Friend connecting with friend. What a priceless moment. How we need moments such as this in our own lives. Our thirsty souls need a drink of God. Our hungry hearts need a belly full of Him.

Let the mountain of the Lord captivate and allure you to its peaks. There you will be taught His ways. There you will cry for change, deep change, change from within that makes you more like God, change that makes you the best you—the you God created you to be.

## GO TO FIND RELIEF

We look at spiritual giants with a skewed perspective. We assume that they were born strong, that they were always powerful, and that they never faced staggering challenges. How much further from the truth could we be?

In his autobiography *Just As I Am* Billy Graham describes one of the times when he sought the Lord for relief. His ministry was at the verge of being shipwrecked. His confidence was almost lost. He writes, "I had to have an answer. If I could not trust the Bible, I could not go on...I got up and took a walk. The moon was out. The shadows were long in the San Bernardino Mountains surrounding the retreat center. Dropping to my knees there in the woods, I opened the Bible at random on a tree stump in front of me...It was an altar where I could only stutter into prayer. The exact wording is beyond recall, but it must have echoed my thoughts, 'O God! There are many things in this book I do not understand. There are many problems with it for which I have no solution. There are many seeming contradictions....Father, I am going to accept this as Thy Word—by faith! I'm going to allow faith to go beyond my intellectual questions and doubts, and I will believe this to be Your inspired Word."[2]

During this time on the mountain, Graham found relief. His time of prayer, confession, soul searching, and self-discovery brought him much-needed mental clarity and inner peace. The internal storm had ended. Within the next twenty-four months he soared to national prominence.

**Find relief from your troubles.**

Elijah did this too! While battling discouragement and depression, the prophet went to the mountain of the Lord seeking relief. Israel's crazy queen, Jezebel, and her equally insane husband, King Ahab, had publicly vowed to kill him within twenty-four hours. Elijah found himself at that place again—a place of loneliness, a place of feeling his prophetic assignment was too much for him.

Think for a moment. Who could counsel the prophet? Another prophet, you say? Perhaps. But what other prophet in his era had a similar platform and spiritual load? None. As Abraham Heschel wrote, "The prophet is a man who feels fiercely. God has thrust a burden upon his soul."[3] Quite often these prophets—of which Elijah is no exception—were not enamored with being a prophet. It was a twenty-four-hour, seven-days-a-week job, which required that they speak for God. Often God's words through them were sharp, opposite to the culture, and certainly not politically correct. It was a lonely job. To top it off, Elijah's prophecy to Israel during the reign of Ahab and Jezebel drew a major backlash. He was to be a dead man within twenty-four hours, Jezebel had barked.

But a prophet is a human being. He is flesh and blood, with all of the needs, aspirations, emotions, and complexities of a man. He's also God's spokesman. Filled with discouragement, Elijah did the only rational thing. He went to Horeb, the mountain of God, to meet with the Lord.

At first he simply complained to God: "I have been very zealous for the LORD God Almighty. The Israelites have rejected your covenant, torn down your altars, and put your prophets to death with the sword. I am the only one left, and now they are trying to kill me too" (1 Kings 19:10). What I love about this passage is the prophet's honesty and vulnerability, though shrouded in a complaint. He lays out his heart without fear of ridicule, rejection, or being misunderstood by God.

Relief can only come with honesty. And where admission of sin followed by repentance is necessary, go for it. Don't hold back! After Elijah poured out his heart, he found relief in the perspective God offered him. The Lord gave him a new assignment. He was to raise up a new leader—Elisha. On the mountain of the Lord, then, we find relief in the most unexpected forms. Whether your pain stems from confusion, dispute, difference of opinion with a loved one or a coworker, or even a personality clash, God will lead you to relief. For Elijah, relief came in his mentoring and developing a younger man to take his place as the nation's prophet. God's solution to rescue the discouraged prophet was ingenious. Elijah's mind moved away from despair and depression when he realized that some unshaped, untrained prophet needed what he had to offer.

**Find relief from difficulties.**

As newlyweds look ahead to their marital future, everything appears rosy and bright, but as life together goes on, trouble often brews. According to Ray his grandparents Amelia and Raul were no exception. They were married in Brooklyn, having emigrated from Puerto Rico, and Amelia had been involved in Santeria—a form of witchcraft. Raul had no problem with that since it didn't interfere with his irreligious lifestyle. In a few years, however, there was trouble in paradise. Amelia met the Savior and fell head over heels in love with Jesus.

Raul became livid. He wanted nothing to do with Christ. In fact, his hatred of God, the Bible, and his wife's newfound faith were so intense that Amelia would have to pray during the night while he slept. Anything related to Christianity, church, or Amelia's salvation drove Raul to mockery and at times hostility. Whenever Amelia attempted to go to church, Raul would physically block her or lock her in the house. After a bout of physical abuse where he pushed her around and roughed her up, Amelia escaped the house. During her time away she decided to really seek God.

She went on an extended time of fasting and prayer to seek relief. This is another thing that going to the mountain is all about. While there, the Lord spoke these words to

Amelia: "Go back to him. I'm going to save him!" She reluctantly obeyed. Armed with that promise from God, Amelia returned home. Raul said, "Go ahead and go to church but don't tell me anything about it." At times he still would mock her, but at no time did he ever again prevent her from going.

Amelia began to take God's promise to the mountain weekly. Seldom did a week go by without her giving to God a day of fasting and much prayer for Raul's conversion. After a few months on the mountaintop Amelia's faith was unshakeable. She kept praying God's promise back to God. After all, God's promise of Raul's salvation was more important to God than to Amelia!

According to Ray, it took more than thirty years of prayer and fasting before Raul came to know Christ. The glorious event of his conversion occurred in October 2002. Talk about mixing faith with patience! Amelia was the poster child of that Hebrews 6:12 principle. But she believed the word God spoke to her on the mountaintop.

When I heard Ray share this story, he told of his own experiences as a child with his grandfather following his conversion. Raul would regularly speak about Jesus and God's love for everybody. There would often be a twinkle in his eyes as he told and retold how God's mercy reached down and changed his cold, sin-hardened heart.

When Raul later fell ill, Amelia took his case to the mountain of the Lord again. After some time God spoke to her: "Let him go. Your prayers are impeding Me from taking him. Let him go. Enough! Stop praying for his healing." Amelia shared the account with her family. They listened. They were comforted. She let him go. God took Raul on January 3, 2003.

The mountain of the Lord is definitely the place where you find relief. But here in America we struggle with this. That's because we want everything yesterday. This is the era of microwave Christianity. Even when it comes to victories, we are almost overbearing when we approach God for help. For some who ascend the mountain of the Lord, they think it's their mountain, not God's. Some act as if they are doing God a favor to even step foot on His mountain. What gall. What nerve. But that's how we are. And to think relief may take time—it's almost sacrilegious to say that out loud. However, the stark reality is that we cannot predict when relief from pain or life's difficulties will occur. Hopefully it won't take more than thirty years as it did in Amelia's situation. In any event, we must be committed to the process of going to the mountain of Lord. Like Abraham, we must declare, "On the mountain of the LORD it will be provided" (Gen. 22:14).

## GO TO RECEIVE YOUR REWARDS

I'm sure you can relate to the time I once received an advertisement in the mail with bold words plastered across the front cover: "Come and claim your prize!" It was from a local car dealership. A car key had been taped to the flyer with a six-digit number below it. To the right of the key was one of those scratch-offs. The instructions read, "Scratch off and see if the revealed number matches the other number. If it does, you've won one of four prizes." Then they showed a new car, a Walmart gift card worth up to $5,000, a $5,000 island vacation, and $50 in cash.

I usually just throw away this type of advertisement. But the appeal of a prize drew me to play their little game.

I scratched off the number and, sure enough, it was a 100 percent match. But I'm far too suspicious, and rightly so, to run down to the dealership and claim my prize. At least one of them belongs to me, so they say. Although I can't read between the lines of the glossy four-color piece, I'm sure their intent was to lure me to the dealership under the pretense of a reward. You know how it goes—we've all been duped into wasting our time chasing after some promise made by a slick marketing campaign.

But when it comes to God and His advertised promises found in sacred Scripture, the thought that you've been duped must never enter your mind. One of the clearest promises in all of Scripture is, "And without faith it is impossible to please God, because anyone who comes to him must believe that he exists and that he *rewards* those who earnestly seek him" (Heb. 11:6, emphasis added).

Did you know that God has an incentive program when it comes to seeking Him? Not only is there an inherent benefit of meeting with God, but He also guarantees you a reward. All are winners—all who scale the mountain of the Lord.

Although the primary focus when seeking God is to hang out with Him, we must not overlook the fact that He promised to reward us. The rewards are the answers to your requests, prayers, and pleas. The reward is the favor of God. The reward is the anointing of God upon your life and business. God's rewards reflect His generous nature. Go to the mountain and let God reward you lavishly.

In *Dynamics of Spiritual Gifts* William McRae shares this example of God's lavish rewards: "When Adoniram Judson graduated from college and seminary he received a call from a fashionable church in Boston to become its assistant pastor. Everyone congratulated him. His mother and sister rejoiced that he could live at home with them and do his life work, but Judson shook his head. 'My work is not here,' he said. 'God is calling me beyond the seas. To stay here, even to serve God in His ministry, I feel would be only partial obedience, and I could not be happy in that.' Although it cost him a great struggle, he left mother and sister to follow the heavenly call. The fashionable church in Boston still stands, rich and strong, but Judson's churches in Burma have 50,000 converts, and the influence of his consecrated life is felt around the world."[4]

If Adoniram Judson had not scaled the mountain of God to inquire of the Lord, what would have become of God's dream for Burma? Throughout his college and seminary training Adoniram made prayer a solid discipline that he learned apart from the normal academic studies. It was in prayer that he felt an inward witness that his destiny was on the mission field. This is why the place of prayer is so critical to our discovery of the will of God. At times you must go to the mountain of the Lord to inquiry of His plans for your life. Settling for the good is not good enough. You must settle for the will of God, which is discovered on the mountain of the Lord.

Like the Colorado Mountains, God's mountain is hypnotic and alluring. Unlike the Glen Eyrie hotel, there is no waiver God wants you to sign that dismisses you from the magnetism of the mountain of the Lord. In fact, just the opposite is true. God invites you to His mountain. He wants you to scale its peaks to meet with Him. Like men and women of old, you'll be better after the climb.

Go ahead! Scale God's mountain. Meet face-to-face with God. Unburden your soul. Pour out your heart. Find relief! Seize your rewards! It's your turn now!

# CONCLUSION

**M**ARTHA NEVER HAD anything negative to say about anyone. She seemed to find a way to be cheerful and upbeat regardless of the circumstance. And Becky was sick of it. Enough already. Martha's unflappable happy disposition and bubbly smile that embraced everyone was getting on Becky's nerves.

Spitefully, Becky blew up and jabbed Martha with a snarky put down. "You've got something good to say about everybody! What would you say about the devil?"

Even as she asked the question in anger, though, Becky's smile never waned. She paused in silence like a winning chess player quietly waits after uttering the game-ending words, "Checkmate!"

But Martha surprised everyone with her true-to-form reply. "You must admit; the devil is quite persistent. He never seems to quit."

Becky walked away, whispering under her breath, "She's right!"

Although this is a cute little story, it mirrors what Peter taught us. This seasoned kneeling warrior advised us, "Be alert and of sober mind. Your enemy the devil prowls around like a roaring lion looking for someone to devour. Resist him, standing firm in the faith, because you know that the family of believers throughout the world is undergoing the same kind of sufferings" (1 Pet. 5:8–9). The spiritual war we're embroiled in never ends while we're in this world. Therefore, we must maintain alertness and vigilance regardless of the number of battles we've fought, won, or even lost. Our faith must stay engaged. Our weapons must stay tuned and ready for immediate use.

We cannot ignore Simon Peter's advice. There is too much at stake.

And he's the perfect salesman to push the use of prayer as a weapon. He could remember back to the onset of his ministry when Satan attacked him—sifting him as wheat, remember? And how Jesus stepped in with a counterattack, saying, "I have prayed for you, Simon" (Luke 22:32). Shortly thereafter Peter was delivered. His ministry was rescued. His legacy was preserved. Satan's plans had failed. Jesus's prayer proved most successful.

So Peter does not speak to us from a theoretical or abstract perspective. He speaks as a benefactor of prayer and as an expert in the use of the weapon of prayer. You cannot argue with a proven practitioner. You simply follow their advice.

Prayer must become the mainstay of your life—for life. Be persistent in prayer! Be vigilant with your life of prayer! There are more battles to be fought. There are more trophies to be won for the kingdom of God.

Even to the very end Jesus was praying—fighting for the souls of the spiritually disconnected. After the trial, the jeering, and the whipping, with arms nailed to the cross and elevated between two criminals, He prayed: "Father, forgive them, for they do not know what they are doing" (Luke 23:34). If our Master was a kneeling warrior through the end, we must be the same!

# NOTES

## INTRODUCTION

1. "Come, My Soul, Thy Suit Prepare" by John Newton. Public domain.

## CHAPTER 1
## YOU MUST FIGHT!

1. Snejana Farberov, "'Why Did No One Come to My Rescue?' Mother Who Survived Savage McDonald's Beating That Was Filmed by Onlookers Speaks Out as Police Hunt for Her Attacker," DailyMail.com, June 27, 2014, http://www .dailymail.co.uk/news/article-2672460/Its-messed-no-one -came-rescue-Mother-survived-savage-beating-captured -viral-video-speaks-time-police-hunt-attacker.html (accessed April 16, 2015).

2. Brainyquote.com, "Martin Luther King Jr. Quotes," http:// www.brainyquote.com/quotes/quotes/m/martinluth103571 .html (accessed April 20, 2015).

3. "Nobel Prize Speech," Wiesel Foundation for Humanity, December 10, 1986, http://www.eliewieselfoundation.org/ nobelprizespeech.aspx (accessed April 20, 2015).

4. E. M. Bounds, *The Weapon of Prayer* (New Kensington, PA: Whitaker House, 1997).

5. NPR News. http://www.npr.org/2014/04/10/300989561/a
-year-after-bombings-some-say-boston-strong-has-gone-over
board (accessed April 20, 2015).

6. *A Few Good Men* directed by Rob Reiner (Culver City, CA:
Sony Pictures Home Entertainment, 2001), DVD.

7. As quoted in Wesley L. Duewel, *Mighty Prevailing Prayer*
(Grand Rapids, MI: Zondervan, 1990).

8. As quoted in William Douglas Chamberlain, *The Meaning of
Repentance* (Philadelphia: Westminster Press, 1943), 23.

9. Charles G. Finney, *Revival Lectures* (Old Tappan, NJ:
Fleming H. Revell Company, n.d.), 121.

## CHAPTER 2
## ONE POWERFUL WEAPON

1. Norval Geldenhuys, *The New International Commentary on
the New Testament: The Gospel of Luke* (Grand Rapids, MI:
Wm. B. Eerdmans Publishing Co., 1988), 566.

2. USLegal.com, "Terroristic Threat Law and Legal Definition,"
http://definitions.uslegal.com/t/terroristic-threat/ (accessed
April 5, 2015).

3. J. H. Jowett, *God—Our Contemporary* (New York: Fleming H.
Revell Co., 1922), 18.

4. Melanie Eversley, "'Angel' Priest Visits Missouri Accident
Scene," USA Today, August 13, 2013, http://www.usatoday
.com/story/news/nation/2013/08/07/angel-crash-missouri
/2630227/ (accessed April 21, 2015).

5. Leonard Ravenhill, *Revival Praying* (Bloomington, MI:
Bethany House, 2005), 33.

6. A. E. Thompson. *A. B. Simpson: His Life and Work* (New
York: Christian Alliance Publishing Company, 1920), 188.

7. Associated Press, "Daredevil Nik Wallenda Completes Tightrope Walk Near Grand Canyon," June 24, 2013, http://www
.foxnews.com/us/2013/06/24/aerialist-wallenda-to-cross
-gorge-near-g-canyon/#ixzz2bZBFAYd9 (accessed April 21,
2015).

8. Ibid.

9. HBO, *Real Sports With Bryant Gumbel*, episode 195, June 25, 2013.

10. James S. Hewett, ed., *Illustrations Unlimited* (Carol Stream, IL: Tyndale House, 1988), 187–188.

## CHAPTER 3
## OUR GOD IS A GENERAL

1. Reena Ninan, "Father Bares Some Skin in Daisy Dukes to Teach Daughter a Lesson," ABC News, September 13, 2013, https://gma.yahoo.com/blogs/abc-blogs/father-bares-skin -daisy-dukes-teach-daughter-lesson-130620319--abc-news -parenting.html (accessed April 21, 2015).

2. Melanie Rudd, Kathleen D. Vohs, and Jennifer Aaker, "Awe Expands People's Perception of Time, Alters Decision Making, and Enhances Well-Being," http://faculty-gsb .stanford.edu/aaker/pages/documents/TimeandAwe2012 _workingpaper.pdf (accessed April 21, 2015).

3. As quoted in Paul Lee Tan, *Encyclopedia of 7700 Illustrations: A Treasury of Illustrations, Anecdotes, Facts and Quotations for Pastors, Teachers, and Christian Workers* (Garland, TX: Bible Communications, 1996).

4. John Owen, *Communion With God* (Carlisle, PA: Banner of Truth Trust, 1991), 31.

5. A. W. Tozer, *The Pursuit of God* (Camp Hill, PA: Christian Publications Inc., 1982), 15.

6. Mark Couvillon, "Fighting Words," in *Christian History*, 1996, http://www.christianitytoday.com/ch/1996/ issue50/5013.html (accessed April 22, 2015).

## CHAPTER 4
## LIFT UP A WAR CRY!

1. As quoted in Larry Kreider, *Building Your Personal House of Prayer* (Shippensburg, PA: Destiny Image Publishers Inc., 2008), 155.

2. As quoted in Mrs. Charles E. Cowman, *Streams in the Desert* (Grand Rapids, MI: Zondervan Publishing, 1965).

3. Charles Spurgeon, *Lectures to My Students* (Grand Rapids, MI: Zondervan, 2010).

4. Leonard Ravenhill, *Why Revival Tarries* (Minneapolis, MN: Bethany House Publishers, 1984), 23.

CHAPTER 5

BE STRATEGIC IN YOUR PRAYER

1. John R. Donahue, *The Gospel in Parable* (Minneapolis, MN: Fortress Press, 1988), 186.

2. "Daredevil Wallenda Becomes First Person to Walk on Tightrope Across Niagara Falls," Fox News, June 15, 2012, http://www.foxnews.com/us/2012/06/15/wallenda-begins-walks-across-niagara-falls-wire/#ixzz1ydUpIEer (accessed April 22, 2015).

3. Sami K. Martin, "Dr. Kent Brantly's Last Sermon Before Contracting Ebola Reveals God's Call on His Life," Christian Post, August 4, 2014, http://www.christianpost.com/news/dr-kent-brantlys-last-sermon-before-contracting-ebola-reveals-gods-call-on-his-life-124263/ (accessed April 22, 2015).

4. "'A Miraculous Day,'" Samaritan's Purse, August 21, 2014, http://www.samaritanspurse.org/article/samaritans-purse-doctor-recovered-from-ebola/ (accessed April 22, 2015).

5. "Dr. Kent Brantly Full Statement," Samaritan's Purse, August 21, 2014, http://www.samaritanspurse.org/article/dr-kent-brantly-full-statement/ (accessed April 22, 2015).

6. Owen, *Communion With God*, 102.

7. Frances Chan, *Crazy Love* (Colorado Spring, CO: David C. Cook, 2013), 68.

## CHAPTER 6
### PRAYER AS DEFENSE

1. As quoted in James W. Bryant and Mac Brunson, *The New Guidebook for Pastors* (Nashville: B&H Publishing Group, 2007).

2. Dr. and Mrs. Howard Taylor, *Hudson Taylor's Spiritual Secret* (New Kensington, PA: Whitaker House, 2003).

3. Ibid., 38–39.

4. Richard C. H. Lenski, *The Interpretation of St. Paul's Epistles to the Colossians and Thessalonians* (Minneapolis, MN: Augsburg Fortress, 2008), 202–204.

5. Richard Stearns, *The Hole in Our Gospel* (Nashville: Thomas Nelson, 2009), 30–34.

6. Billy Graham, *Just As I Am* (New York: HarperCollins, 2007), 257.

7. Ibid., 258.

8. Ibid., 259.

9. Ibid.

10. Spurgeon, *Lectures to My Students*.

## CHAPTER 7
### PRAYER AS OFFENSE

1. Ravenhill, *Revival Praying*, 125.

2. Tan, *Encyclopedia of 7,700 Illustrations*.

3. Hewett, *Illustrations Unlimited*, 425.

4. As quoted in Charles H. Spurgeon, "A Lecture for Little-Faith," in *Faith in All Its Splendor* (N.p.: Sovereign Grace Publishers, 2006), 11.

5. Positiveprayers.com, "Famous Prayer Quotes," http://www.positiveprayers.com/famous-prayer-quotes.html (accessed May 13, 2015).

6. "Superstar Interview: Michael Phelps," Parenting.com, http://www.parenting.com/article/superstar-interview-michael-phelps (accessed April 23, 2015).

7. Thinkexist.com, "Aristotle Quotes," http://thinkexist.com/quotation/man_is_a_goal_seeking_animal-his_life_only_has/297104.html (accessed April 23, 2015).

8. Rob Gilbert, ed., *Bits and Pieces* (Fairfield, New Jersey: The Economics Press, Inc., Vol. T/No. 15), 9–11.

9. Tozer, *Pursuit of God.*

## CHAPTER 8
### WHAT'S YOUR RANK, SOLDIER?

1. As quoted in John Maxwell and Jim Dornan, *How to Influence People* (Nashville: Thomas Nelson, 2013), 36.

2. Goodreads.com, "Ralph Waldo Emerson Quotes," http://www.goodreads.com/quotes/74783-what-i-need-is-someone-who-will-make-me-do (accessed April 23, 2015).

3. James S. Hewett, *Illustrations Unlimited*, 424.

4. "Geico Pinocchio Bad Motivational Speaker Commercial," Marketmenot.com, http://www.marketmenot.com/geico-pinocchio-bad-motivational-speaker-commercial/ (accessed April 23, 2015).

5. David Bennett, *William Booth* (Bloomington, MI: Bethany House, 1994), 128–130.

6. "This Day in History: 1954 First Four-Minute Mile," History.com, http://www.history.com/this-day-in-history/first-four-minute-mile (accessed April 23, 2015); Richard Cavendish, "The First Sub-Four-Minute Mile," *History Today*, May 2004, http://www.historytoday.com/richard-cavendish/first-sub-four-minute-mile (accessed April 23, 2015).

7. "Matt Sloane, Jason Hanna, and Dana Ford, "Never, Ever Give Up: Diana Nyad Completes Historic Cuba-to-Florida Swim," CNN, September 3, 2013, http://www.cnn.com/2013/09/02/world/americas/diana-nyad-cuba-florida-swim/ (accessed April 23, 2015).

8. John Pollock, *The Billy Graham Story* (Grand Rapids, MI: Zondervan, 2003), 24.

## CHAPTER 9
## THE MOUNTAIN OF THE LORD

1. Tozer, *Pursuit of God*, 15.

2. Graham, *Just As I Am*.

3. Abraham J. Heschel, *The Prophets* (New York: HarperCollins, 2001), 5.

4. William McRae, *Dynamics of Spiritual Gifts* (Grand Rapids, MI: Zondervan, 1976).

# ABOUT THE AUTHOR

D R. DAVID IRELAND is founder and senior pastor of Christ Church in Montclair, New Jersey, an eight thousand-member congregation of forty nationalities. Diversity consultant to the National Basketball Association, Dr. Ireland leads chapel services for the New York Giants, New York Jets, and at the US Pentagon. Author of approximately twenty books, Ireland has appeared on *The Dr. Phil Show*, the *CBS Evening News*, and *The 700 Club*. Through his community development corporation he offers a home for victims of domestic violence and a youth leadership institute. Dr. Ireland holds an undergraduate degree in mechanical engineering (Fairleigh Dickinson University), a graduate degree in civil engineering (Stevens Institute of Technology), and a master's degree in theology (Alliance Theological Seminary). He has an earned doctorate degree in organizational leadership (Regent University) and has completed postdoctoral work at the University of Pennsylvania. Dr. Ireland was recently appointed as a member of the Governor's Advisory Commission on Faith-Based Initiatives. He also serves on the boards of Nyack College and Alliance Theological Seminary and was an adjunct professor at Drew University. He and his wife, Marlinda, have been married since 1984 and have two adult daughters. To learn more visit www.DavidIreland.org.